T0303270

Building the Best Offensive and Defensive Cyber Workforce

Volume II, Attracting and Retaining Enlisted and Civilian Personnel

CHAITRA M. HARDISON, LESLIE ADRIENNE PAYNE, JULIA WHITAKER, ANTHONY LAWRENCE, IVICA PAVISIC

Prepared for the Department of the Air Force
Approved for public release; distribution unlimited

PROJECT AIR FORCE

For more information on this publication, visit **www.rand.org/t/RRA1056-2**.

About RAND

The RAND Corporation is a research organization that develops solutions to public policy challenges to help make communities throughout the world safer and more secure, healthier and more prosperous. RAND is nonprofit, nonpartisan, and committed to the public interest. To learn more about RAND, visit www.rand.org.

Research Integrity

Our mission to help improve policy and decisionmaking through research and analysis is enabled through our core values of quality and objectivity and our unwavering commitment to the highest level of integrity and ethical behavior. To help ensure our research and analysis are rigorous, objective, and nonpartisan, we subject our research publications to a robust and exacting quality-assurance process; avoid both the appearance and reality of financial and other conflicts of interest through staff training, project screening, and a policy of mandatory disclosure; and pursue transparency in our research engagements through our commitment to the open publication of our research findings and recommendations, disclosure of the source of funding of published research, and policies to ensure intellectual independence. For more information, visit www.rand.org/about/principles.

RAND's publications do not necessarily reflect the opinions of its research clients and sponsors.

Published by the RAND Corporation, Santa Monica, Calif.
© 2021 RAND Corporation
RAND® is a registered trademark.

Library of Congress Cataloging-in-Publication Data is available for this publication.
ISBN: 978-1-9774-0786-3

Cover: Airman 1st Class Krystal Ardrey/Air Force.

About This Report

The U.S. military's success in cyberwarfare hinges in part on the capabilities of the cyber personnel the military brings to the fight. Given that cyberwarfare is considered a core element of the U.S. Air Force (USAF) mission and a core capability that USAF provides to combatant commanders, USAF needs to ensure that its personnel are trained and developed in a way that best suits the cyber mission. With this in mind, USAF has been looking for ways to revamp and improve the training and development of its offensive and defensive cyberwarfare workforce to develop the best fighting force possible. USAF is also cognizant of the importance of recruiting and retention in realizing the full potential of any training and development efforts and has sought to better understand some of the drivers of attraction to and retention in the cyber field.

This report, the second of two volumes, summarizes RAND Project AIR FORCE's work exploring the views of the enlisted and civilian workforce on these topics. Our study builds upon similar recent RAND Corporation work focused on understanding the views of the officer cyber workforce (see Hardison et al., 2019). The results from this study are intended to inform policymaker decisions about changes to USAF offensive and defensive cyber training and development efforts, as well as USAF efforts to recruit and retain the best personnel for the job. In this volume, we present our findings on recruiting and retention; in Volume I, we present our findings on training and development (Hardison et al., 2021). Some of the material presented in this volume—such as the impetus for our research and our overall approach—is repeated in Hardison et al., 2021. This report should interest cyber community leadership, USAF and U.S. Department of Defense leaders concerned with the management of the cyber workforce and the effectiveness of the cyber warfare mission more broadly, and USAF and U.S. Department of Defense senior leaders responsible for managing USAF career fields.

The research reported here was commissioned by the Secretary of the Air Force, Office of the Assistant Deputy Chief Information Officer for Digital Transformation and Assistant Deputy Chief of Staff for Cyber Effects Operations, and conducted within the Workforce, Development, and Health Program of RAND Project AIR FORCE as part of a fiscal year 2019 project, *Building and Retaining a Military Cyber Force*.

RAND Project AIR FORCE

RAND Project AIR FORCE (PAF), a division of the RAND Corporation, is the Department of the Air Force's (DAF's) federally funded research and development center for studies and analyses, supporting both the United States Air Force and the United States Space Force. PAF provides the DAF with independent analyses of policy alternatives affecting the development, employment, combat readiness, and support of current and future air, space, and cyber forces.

Research is conducted in four programs: Strategy and Doctrine; Force Modernization and Employment; Workforce, Development, and Health; and Resource Management. The research reported here was prepared under contract FA7014-16-D-1000.

Additional information about PAF is available on our website: www.rand.org/paf/

This report documents work originally shared with the DAF on September 26, 2019. The draft report, issued on September 30, 2019, was reviewed by formal peer reviewers and DAF subject-matter experts.

Contents

Figures

Tables

Summary

Issue

Cyberwarfare is considered a core element of the U.S. Air Force (USAF) mission. People with cybersecurity skill sets are in great demand, not only in the military but also in the private sector. As a result, USAF is concerned that recruiting and retaining talented cyber personnel might be increasingly difficult. Thus, USAF expressed an interest in better understanding the perspectives of members of its cyber workforce and the insights that could be gained from their views. USAF turned to RAND Project AIR FORCE for assistance in gathering these insights. Prior RAND work explored these issues among officers; this report focuses on enlisted and civilian members of the cyber workforce.

Approach

We conducted 30 focus groups and interviews to collect the viewpoints of cyber enlisted and civilian personnel in offensive and defensive cyber operations—specifically the cyber warfare operations (1B4) specialty, digital network analyst (1N4A) specialty, and civilians operating as part of the cyber mission force (CMF). We also reviewed USAF's archival personnel data files to examine retention profiles for the civilian and enlisted cyber workforce.

Conclusions

- Participants had mixed views on whether recruiting was a concern. In 43 percent of focus groups, at least one participant said that there were recruiting challenges; however, in 63 percent of focus groups, at least one participant said that there were not recruiting challenges.

  – Questionnaire respondents responded neutrally on the question of satisfaction with the level of cyber talent being recruited.

- In contrast, participants in 77 percent of focus groups said that retention is a concern (Figure S.1).

  – Participants explained that they were less concerned with retention overall. Instead, they were concerned that the *best-quality* personnel were the ones leaving.

- Consistent with this finding, the personnel data that we reviewed suggest that cyber retention overall is not a problem. However, our analysis of Armed Forces Qualification Test scores lends support to participants' concerns that the best people might be leaving at higher rates than other cyber personnel.

Recommendations

- **Track and monitor retention, especially of top performers.** Currently, there is no systematic way to identify or track top performers, but USAF should begin collecting such data to track retention.
- **Develop materials to help get recruiters and the public well versed in cyber career fields.** Develop materials that can be used to better explain the job to a lay audience and the overall criticality of the cyber mission to USAF. The materials should provide a realistic preview of the job, including the skill, ability, and interest requirements.
- **Truncate the onboarding process for civilians.** Revisit the merits of the 180-day processing period for applicants with prior USAF service with cyber backgrounds who wish to come back as civilian cyber specialists. Explore whether financial compensation could be given to viable applicants during the clearance process.
- **Create senior technical (nonmanagement) roles.** Some cyber personnel want the ability to "stay on keyboard" indefinitely to maintain their technical skills and do the work that they enjoy instead of being forced to assume supervisory roles via promotion. A warrant officer track would address this; other technical track solutions could also be considered.
- **Take steps to address bureaucracy and other major sources of dissatisfaction.** USAF needs to address these frustrating obstacles to counter the draw of the private sector and ensure that these obstacles do not continue as the enterprise normalizes.
- **Improve identification and tracking of civilians in the CMF.** The Air Force Personnel Center currently does not have a clear way of identifying civilians in the CMF. This is a necessary first step to monitor retention of these individuals.

Figure S.1. Percentage of Focus Groups That Mentioned Specific Topics About Retention

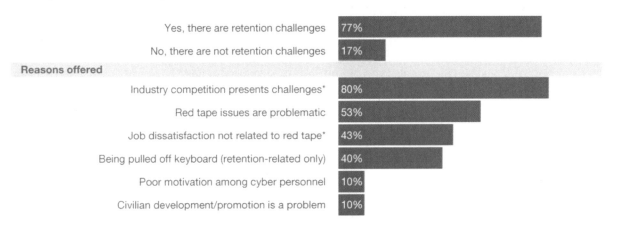

NOTE: Some focus groups had only one participant, meaning that they were essentially interviews. These interviews are included in the focus group results shown in this figure. Sometimes, a topic was raised by one person, and an opposite view was expressed by someone in the same focus group. In those cases, the same discussion would be counted in both the topic frequency and the opposite sentiment frequency. For some topics, no opposite sentiment was expressed in the workforce discussions. When an opposite sentiment was expressed in more than 7 percent of the workforce discussions, it was added to the figure. Where an opposite sentiment was expressed in 3 to 7 percent of the workforce focus groups (i.e., one or two groups), the category is marked with an asterisk. Being pulled off keyboard was also mentioned in our Volume I results as a potential training issue (e.g., not being on keyboard results in loss of skill currency). Being pulled off keyboard was also discussed in the context of retention, and those comments were coded separately.

Acknowledgments

We would like to acknowledge several people who contributed to this work. First, we thank Maj Gen Kevin Kennedy, Assistant Deputy Chief Information Officer for Digital Transformation and Assistant Deputy Chief of Staff for Cyber Effects Operations, for his guidance and input over the course of the project. We thank our study point of contact, Col Bobby Thompson, for his insights and assistance in developing and scoping the work. We also thank Danielle Vann and Lt Col Mary King from our sponsor's office for their assistance in identifying and contacting the various training subject-matter experts (SME) who participated in our study.

We are grateful to several key individuals at the RAND Corporation who contributed to the study. Sarah Soliman, an integral member of the team, contributed ideas over the course of the project, led focus groups at one military base location, and participated in several of the SME discussions. Col Katrina (KT) Terry, who also served as an important member of the team, assisted in the project during her year serving as an Air Force Fellow at RAND by participating in team meetings and offering feedback on the questionnaire items, the focus group discussion questions, the SMEs and bases being targeted, and other aspects of the overall study design and scope. In addition, we thank our peer reviewers, Caolionn O'Connell, Jeffrey Kendall, and Maria Lytell.

Lastly, and most importantly, this study would not have been possible without the assistance from our base points of contact and the participants themselves. Our base points of contact graciously gave their time to plan out and coordinate the visits, scheduled conference rooms for us to hold our discussions, reached out to members of the workforce to let them know about the focus groups and to encourage participation, and checked in on and escorted us as needed throughout our visits. It is because of them that our visits were successful. We are also grateful to all of the people who volunteered to participate in our study (SMEs and workforce members alike) and took time out of their busy schedules to share their views on the workforce's recruiting and retention challenges.

Abbreviations

AFPC	Air Force Personnel Center
AFQT	Armed Forces Qualification Test
BRS	Blended Retirement System
CMF	cyber mission force
CNMF	Cyber National Mission Force
DCO	defensive cyber operations
DoD	U.S. Department of Defense
DoDIN	Department of Defense Information Network
GS	general schedule
IT	information technology
JBSA	Joint Base San Antonio
OCO	offensive cyber operations
SME	subject-matter expert
USAF	U.S. Air Force

1. Introduction

The U.S. military's success in cyberwarfare hinges in part on the capabilities of the cyber personnel the military brings to the fight. Given that cyberwarfare is considered a core element of the U.S. Air Force (USAF) mission and a core capability that USAF provides to combatant commanders, USAF needs to ensure that its personnel are trained and developed in a way that best suits the cyber mission. With this in mind, USAF has been looking for ways to revamp and improve the training and development of its offensive and defensive cyberwarfare workforce to develop the best fighting force possible. USAF is also cognizant of the importance of recruiting and retention in realizing the full potential of any training and development efforts and has sought to better understand some of the drivers of attraction to and retention in the cyber field.[1]

This report, the second of two volumes, summarizes RAND Project AIR FORCE's work exploring the views of the enlisted and civilian workforce on these topics. This study builds upon similar recent RAND Corporation work that focused on understanding the views of the officer cyber workforce (see Hardison et al., 2019).[2] The results of our study are intended to inform policymaker decisions about changes to USAF offensive and defensive cyber training and development efforts, as well as USAF efforts to recruit and retain the best personnel for the job. In this volume, we present our findings on recruiting and retention; in Volume I, we present our findings on training and development.

---

[1] This section also appears in Hardison et al., 2021.

[2] Note that the cyber workforce community encompasses a much larger set of personnel than just those explored in this study. Within USAF, the cyber workforce includes additional enlisted career fields, such as the 3DXs (the cyberspace support career fields), officers, other members of the civilian workforce, and USAF reserve and guard personnel. Unfortunately, because of resource constraints, we were unable to explore all of these workforces in this study. Instead, to fit within our study budget, the sponsor scoped this effort to focus just on active-duty 1N4As (digital network analysts) and 1B4s (cyber warfare operations personnel).

However, the sponsor also acknowledged that there was interest in exploring these issues in the reserve and guard communities and in the other enlisted career fields (such as the 3DXs) and that there would be benefits in doing so. In addition, a view of these issues with the total force in mind might provide different insights and solutions. For example, the ability for reservists and guardsmen to work in the private-sector cyber field, attain additional certifications, and stay technically current while still having the opportunity to engage in military offensive cyber operations (OCO)–type work might be especially attractive for some personnel.

Lastly, it is worth noting that the study was scoped to focus only on training and recruiting issues in USAF, but much of the cyber work and training being conducted exist in a joint environment and many of the issues might be shared across the services. Therefore, a joint view of these issues could be worthwhile. Although we approach enlisted cyber workforce issues in this report from a USAF perspective only, these issues are in fact U.S. Department of Defense (DoD)–wide challenges. Given the joint, interagency, allied, and coalition operating environments that depends on cyber as a crosscutting domain, this force-wide view might be especially important in understanding cyber workforce issues.

Why Recruiting and Retention Are Worth Exploring

People with cybersecurity skill sets are in great demand, not only in the military and within other government agencies but also in the private sector. However, unlike the private sector, USAF is limited in the types of incentives it can offer its cyber workforce. As a result, USAF might be at a disadvantage when competing with the private sector for highly competent cyber personnel. This has led many to worry that talented USAF civilian and enlisted cyber personnel might be in short supply and that an inability to recruit and retain talented personnel could further exacerbate the problem. However, much of these concerns are based on speculation and individual anecdotes (e.g., someone tells a story about a fantastic performer who left). Evidence to back up the speculation about recruiting and retention concerns is lacking.

Data provided by the Air Force Personnel Center (AFPC) suggest that retention numbers in these occupations (at least the enlisted ones)[3] are not particularly concerning. Data also show that accession targets are being met. However, these numbers alone cannot address concerns about whether the best personnel are the ones leaving or whether the right people are being attracted to the cyber career field. Nor can data alone indicate whether retention or recruiting concerns are something to keep a close eye on as a potential future issue for the career field.

If the concerns expressed by some are founded, a better understanding of the variety of drivers of recruitment and retention of talented personnel could be critical to combating potential personnel shortages now or in the future.

Goals of This Study

Maj Gen Kevin Kennedy (Assistant Deputy Chief Information Officer for Digital Transformation and Assistant Deputy Chief of Staff for Cyber Effects Operations) asked RAND to conduct a study exploring the cyber workforce's views on changes to training and development that might be beneficial for improving the cyber workforce. In addition, because recruiting and retention are also central to maintaining a capable cyber workforce, he asked that we briefly explore the workforce's views on whether recruiting and retention are concerns in the 1B4 and 1N4A communities. We focused our efforts on exploring the workforce's views on the following broad questions:

- What are the key drivers that cause personnel in the 1B4 and 1N4A cyber workforces to want to stay or leave?

---

[3] To our knowledge, AFPC has not explored retention estimates for the cyber mission force (CMF) civilian workforce. We did consider exploring civilian retention data in this study ourselves, but we had difficulty identifying which civilians were CMF civilians using information available in the existing data records. In addition, there is no consensus on an approach for benchmarking or evaluating civilian retention levels, since civilians can enter laterally at any level, stay for any length of time, leave, and return. As a result, we cannot comment on whether retention numbers would be considered a concern for civilian personnel in the cyber workforce.

- What are the key drivers of personnel's attraction or lack of attraction to these career fields?
- What could USAF do to attract and retain the best cyber personnel?

Drawing on the comments of members of the workforce, we offer options for changes that USAF could consider to help attract and retain cyber personnel.

Our Study Approach

In discussion with our sponsor, we scoped this effort to focus on enlisted and civilian cyber personnel.[4] We explored both the OCO and defensive cyber operations (DCO) workforces, specifically enlisted cyber warfare operations personnel (1B4s) and digital network analysts (1N4As)[5] who work in the OCO or DCO cyber domains.[6] Also included in the scope of our effort were all civilians operating as part of the CMF. Within the 1B and 1N4A career fields, personnel working to build and maintain various aspects of the DoD Information Network (DoDIN) (i.e., personnel whose roles are similar to an information technology [IT] workforce in the private sector) were not included in this study's scope.[7]

We excluded consideration of officers because officers were a focus of a similar research effort two years prior to this study, the results of which informed several recommendations that the sponsor's office was currently executing (see Hardison et al., 2019). In that same study, enlisted and civilian personnel in the cyber workforce were mentioned by participants as additional groups whose viewpoints were also worth exploring, and both were of direct interest to the sponsor's office as groups on which more-systematic research would be worthwhile.

The bulk of our approach relied on focus groups to collect viewpoints from these cyber personnel on drivers of attraction and retention of talent to the cyber career fields. We also interviewed key USAF cyber training and development subject-matter experts (SMEs) and stakeholders (including the career-field managers, cyber training squadron commanders, and

---

[4] This section also appears in Hardison et al., 2021.

[5] We use 1N4A in this report to refer to personnel in Air Force Specialty Code 1N4X1A (i.e., 1N4s who are in the A shred).

[6] It is important to note that the 1N4X1A career field is not under the functional authority of the study sponsor. 1N4X1A does not typically align under OCO/DCO, but rather as cyber mission force (CMF) missions, non-CMF USAF missions, and Combat Support Agency missions. DCO missions for 1N4X1A are limited. The study scope included only those 1B4X1 and 1N4X1A who are participating in the DCO and OCO missions. This reflects most of the 1B4 community but only a subset of the 1N4As.

[7] This should not be taken to suggest that the sponsor's office was not interested in improving training and development in the DoDIN workforce as well, but, because of funding constraints, we could focus on only a subset of the cyber workforce in this study.

personnel overseeing cyber training at Air University and the U.S. Air Force Academy) to identify their views on recruiting and retention in cyber career fields.[8]

The SME and stakeholder discussions focused most heavily on the training questions addressed in Volume I; however, we did invite those SMEs to also offer their comments and insights on recruiting and retention issues. To the extent that they were relevant, those views were incorporated into the results presented in this report.[9] Lastly, we explored USAF's archival personnel data files to see whether retention profiles for civilian and enlisted cyber personnel currently appear problematic.

We chose focus groups and interviews as our primary study approach because our sponsor was particularly interested in the views of the workforce on drivers of recruiting and retention. Focus groups can be especially useful for this type of research goal for two reasons. First, they are useful as an exploratory tool to capture a wide variety of ideas and viewpoints, including ideas that might not have been previously considered. Second, they are useful to help better understand those ideas because researchers are able to probe for more details and ask for additional explanation. In this way, focus groups can provide both a variety of information and a depth of understanding of the issues that other approaches might not.

Focus Group and Interview Participants and Questionnaire Respondents

To collect data on the workforce's views, we visited three military bases (Fort Meade, Maryland; Joint Base San Antonio [JBSA], Texas; and Scott Air Force Base, Illinois). These military bases were chosen because they reflect bases with high concentrations of 1B4s or 1N4As involved in OCO and DCO, which would provide a good overview of viewpoints in the career fields of interest. As shown in Table 1.1, these three bases account for the majority of 1B4s, and two of them account for more than half of the 1N4As.[10]

---

[8] In addition to talking with USAF cyber SMEs, we had hoped to speak with cyber representatives from the other services. However, interviews external to USAF have to be approved through a separate set of offices within DoD, and that approval process would have exceeded our timeline for the project. However, we did interview a few RAND SMEs who have extensive expertise in cyber issues among the U.S. Army and U.S. Navy cyber workforces to determine whether there might be any notable insights or lessons learned by these other services that could help inform our recommendations to USAF. What we learned from those discussions suggested that the other services are facing similar challenges relating to recruiting, retention, and training of cyber personnel and that they, too, are still looking for answers to address those challenges. There were no additional notable insights from those discussions.

[9] Details on the SME participants are contained in Volume I.

[10] Because of the complexities in trying to identify OCO and DCO civilians, we were not able to provide a similar table showing the distribution across bases for personnel in the cyber civilian workforce.

Table 1.1. Distribution of Personnel in the 1N4A and 1B4 Career Fields

| | Personnel | |
Base	1B4	1N4A
Grand total	809	990
Bases visited		
Fort Meade	74	266
JBSA	465	239
Scott Air Force Base	75	5
Total	614	510
Bases not visited		
Fort Gordon	12	65
Goodfellow Air Force Base	0	138
Hickam Air Force Base	27	77
Hurlburt Field	18	6
Keesler Air Force Base	23	0
Naval Air Station Pensacola Corry Station	0	135
Nellis Air Force Base	19	4
Peterson Air Force Base	15	3
Bases with fewer than ten 1B4s or 1N4As	81	52
Total	195	480

NOTE: These data come from the authors' analysis of the September 30, 2019, monthly extract of the Military Personnel Data System.

We held a total of 30 focus group discussions or interviews with members of the workforce,[11] which included a total of 68 enlisted personnel and seven civilians. As shown in Figure 1.1, the number of discussions varied by location: 12 each at Fort Meade and JBSA, five at Scott Air Force Base, and one by phone with a participant who was stationed at another location.[12]

At each location, we held discussions separately by work role (OCO or DCO), by pay grade grouping (senior noncommissioned officer versus noncommissioned officer, general schedule [GS]-11/12/13 versus GS-14/15), and by specialty type (civilian, enlisted 1B4, and enlisted 1N4A). Discussions were approximately evenly split between OCO and DCO work roles, and the overwhelming majority of the discussions were with enlisted 1B4s. The number of participants per discussion varied, ranging from one to seven, but, in most groups, we had two to three participants. Table 1.2 also shows the overall numbers of participants by type of group.[13]

During the focus groups, we administered a questionnaire that included both open-ended questions for write-in responses and questionnaire items to which participants responded using

---

[11] For simplicity's sake, we will use the term *focus group* throughout the report to refer to both focus groups and interviews with members of the cyber workforce. See Volume I for more information on focus group participants.

[12] Note that a few discussions with participants were held by phone to accommodate participants who volunteered but were unavailable to meet with us during our visit.

[13] Note that the numbers of 1B4s and 1N4As who participated reflect close to 7 percent and 5 percent, respectively, of these populations at the three bases (see Table 1.1).

five-point Likert scales (strongly agree to strongly disagree).[14] Those items are explained throughout the report where those results are discussed. Open-ended focus group discussion questions were as follows:

- Do you think there is a problem attracting personnel in your specialty? Why or why not?
- Do you think there is a problem retaining personnel in your specialty? Why or why not?

Open-ended questionnaire questions were as follows:

- What do you like most about your job?
- What do you like least about your job?

A range of additional Likert-scale questions asked participants to rate their satisfaction with various aspects of their jobs. The wording of each of these Likert-scale items is provided throughout this report at the points at which those items are discussed.

In addition to the focus groups, we held a discussion at each base that included one or more leaders (e.g., an officer, a superintendent, someone generally overseeing the officer workforce). The goals of these discussions were threefold: (1) for us to provide background to them about the purpose and goals of the study, (2) for us to learn more about cyber and the cyber personnel at their base, and (3) for us to gather unique insights that they might have on the topics of training, recruiting, and retention. At one base, we held two such discussions; at the others, we held one.[15] These discussions were useful in that leadership's views contributed to some example comments provided through this report and to our understanding of the issues.[16] However, the figures presented throughout the report focus solely on the results from our discussions with cyber personnel.

We also held 12 discussions by phone with stakeholders and SMEs with knowledge and experience in training. The SME and stakeholder participants are described further in Volume I. As with the leadership discussions, we did not include their responses in the results presented in the figures throughout the report. However, their insights were useful in providing context about recruiting and retention issues.

---

[14] We included some items that were similar to or identical to items used in other surveys of USAF personnel (e.g., the Federal Employee Viewpoint Survey and the USAF climate surveys).

[15] The number of discussions held was determined by leaders' availability. At one base, the relevant leadership participants were not available at the same time and therefore were scheduled for separate discussions.

[16] Leadership did not raise any notable issues that were not also raised by members of the workforce.

Figure 1.1. Number of Focus Groups, by Base, Work Role, and Specialty

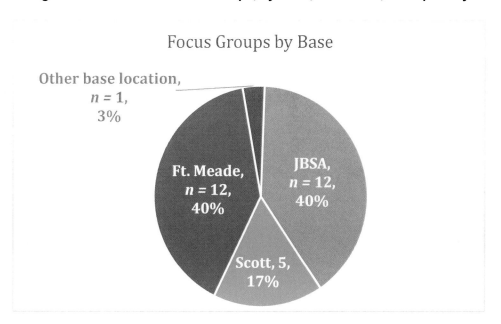

Focus Groups by Base

Other base location, *n* = 1, 3%

Ft. Meade, *n* = 12, 40%

JBSA, *n* = 12, 40%

Scott, 5, 17%

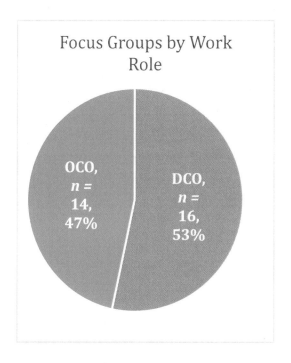

Focus Groups by Work Role

OCO, *n* = 14, 47%

DCO, *n* = 16, 53%

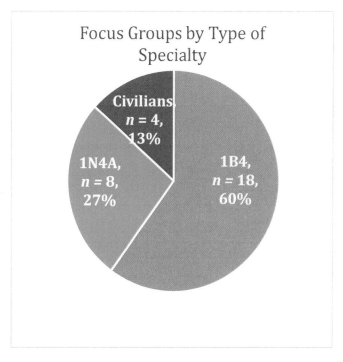

Focus Groups by Type of Specialty

Civilians, *n* = 4, 13%

1N4A, *n* = 8, 27%

1B4, *n* = 18, 60%

Table 1.2. Total Number of Focus Group Participants

Type of Discussion	Number of Participants
By specialty	
1B4	45
1N4A	23
Civilians	7
By work role	
DCO	34
OCO	41
By base[a]	
Fort Meade	39
JBSA	17
Scott Air Force Base	18
Total sample	75

NOTES: Number per group is lower for JBSA in part because we held additional discussions by phone with a few participants who could not attend during our visit. Those phone discussions were held as interviews with one person per discussion.
[a] One phone interview participant was not located at any of the three bases we visited. The total number of participants at the three bases was 74.

We present our results in three ways. First, we present figures summarizing the number of focus groups during which particular comments about recruiting and retention were mentioned to give a sense of the relative frequency of a particular sentiment. For simplicity, we present these results as *overall* focus group percentages, regardless of whether the discussion was with 1B4s, 1N4As, or civilians (percentages within each specialty can be found in Volume I).[17] Second, we intersperse results from our focus group questionnaire to provide further context on participants' views on these topics. Third, we provide comments that illustrate the variety of sentiments offered on these topics and note any differences in the comments observed across the specialties.

---

[17] We present responses together in the main body of the report for a few reasons. First, our sample size for civilians was too small to determine whether meaningful differences in viewpoints existed between the civilian and enlisted groups. In addition, the work performed by the civilian workforce is similar enough to that of the 1N4A and 1B4 workforces that some of their sources of satisfaction or dissatisfaction with the job that might drive retention might be similar in many cases and any differences observed might be simply caused by chance because of the small sample sizes. We discuss this issue more in Appendix E. Recruiting challenges might be more likely to differ, however, and we note those (and any other) qualitative differences that were observed in the text. Likewise, we note instances in which 1B4 and 1N4A comments were noticeably different from each other. The 1N4A sample size was larger than that of the civilians, but the number of focus groups (eight) was still too small to draw definitive conclusions about differences in the numbers of focus groups mentioning a topic. We therefore decided to report the overall focus group counts and address obvious differences in our discussion of the results.

SME or stakeholder comments, although not included in the quantitative data figures in the report, are incorporated into some of the sections for additional context.

A Note About Some Key Differences in Recruiting and Retention of Civilians, 1N4As, and 1B4s

When we conducted this study, we recognized in advance that each of these occupational specialties might face unique challenges with recruiting and retention because the work they do and the policies that affect them might differ. The following are a few examples of some important differences.

In general, USAF hiring and retention of enlisted and civilian personnel differ in some meaningful ways. Enlisted personnel agree to a service commitment of typically four to six years. The length of the service commitment can vary depending on several factors (e.g., the amount of training provided in a given career field, bonuses accepted at the time of enlistment, the choice to enter the service at a higher pay grade, whether the career field is high-demand). Some personnel enlist knowing what career field they will be entering (and, in some cases, are guaranteed that career field), while others join without knowing to what career field they will be assigned, and USAF places them based on their skills, interests, and the needs of USAF. Enlisted personnel are moved to new assignments periodically over the course of their service, and those new assignments are typically located at a different base location. Enlisted personnel also are considered for promotions based in part on their time in grade and time in service. That is, after a specified period of time, personnel are automatically considered for promotion, and promotion eventually becomes a requirement of continued service.

Civilian hiring, by contrast, does not come with a service commitment. Civilians are at-will employees who are free to join USAF or leave it at any time. Promotion to higher pay levels is not obligatory, and such promotions can occur on widely varying timelines (i.e., decisions are not dependent on time spent at a particular pay scale). Civilians can apply to skip ahead multiple pay grades, or they can opt to stay at a given pay grade indefinitely. Entry points of personnel also vary drastically from person to person. Some people enter civilian jobs at lower pay scales and move up the pay grades over time. Others enter at much higher pay grades.[18] This means that the ages of civilian personnel are much more varied at any given pay scale than would be seen at enlisted grades. Some civilian jobs are filled by retired officers or enlisted personnel who have decades of experience in the service, some are filled by officers and enlisted personnel who separated much earlier in their military careers, and some are filled by personnel who have no military background at all.

Another key difference between enlisted and civilian jobs is that civilians are not asked to move assignments or base locations. Civilians are hired for a specific position and stay in that

---

[18] For more on civilian pay, see the U.S. Office of Personnel Management website (U.S. Office of Personnel Management, undated).

position for the duration of their job. This provides for a level of stability and predictability in the civilian positions that does not exist in enlisted roles.[19]

In addition, there are specific rules mandated by federal hiring policies for how civilian jobs can be posted, how qualifications can be evaluated, the onboarding process, and more requirements that USAF must follow. These rules put some significant restrictions on civilian hiring for the cyber workforce that are not a factor in the hiring of enlisted personnel. We discuss a few of these hiring restrictions at the points at which they are relevant later in our report.

Lastly, there is an important difference between 1B4 and 1N4A recruitment that is worth noting at the outset. As with most enlisted occupations, 1N4As are typically assigned to the career field at the start of their USAF careers. For 1B4s, however, recruitment has until recently occurred very differently. Until 2019, the 1B4 career field was cross-train-only, meaning that personnel were allowed to enter only after they had served in another USAF career for some period of time.[20] As a result, entry-level 1B4s all began their cyber careers at much higher grades than entry-level 1N4As. The grade of entry for 1B4s also was variable. Some personnel volunteered to cross-train much later in their USAF careers than other personnel did, meaning that years of 1B4 cyber experience cannot be determined by their rank or years of service alone. The fact that the 1B4 career field has historically been cross-train-only but is no longer has implications for both how personnel are recruited for the career field and their retention behaviors. Some of these implications are noted and discussed at various points later in this report.

Data Limitations and Implications

Several limitations to the data and results are important context for our findings and recommendations. First, the views of our focus group participants might not reflect the views of the entire workforce because our participants come from select bases (not a random sample) and they volunteered to participate.

Second, we largely assume that our participants' views are correct; however, it is possible that they could be inaccurate. For example, it is possible that training problems exist in different forms or to varying degrees from what was expressed by participants. With this in mind, leadership should consider whether additional data collection efforts might be needed prior to implementing a recommendation.

Third, our sample size for each specialty was small for all of the groups, but especially for the civilian workforce (seven participants in four discussions). Therefore, the results for that

---

[19] Civilians can, of course, apply to positions at other bases if they want to move, but that would be akin to leaving one job and taking a completely new one.

[20] See Bui, 2019. Until the change in policy in 2019, personnel were recruited to cross-train into cyber from a wide variety of career fields, and anyone who was eligible to apply could cross-train into it. Now, personnel are allowed to enter into 1B4 training without having to serve in another career field first.

group, in particular, should be evaluated with strong caution because there are likely issues unique to that workforce that we were unable to capture or report.

Fourth, throughout the report, we present the proportion of groups in which at least one participant expressed a particular view or comment, and we discuss the comments in depth that were raised most frequently. However, it is important to point out that some comments might be widely held but still mentioned less frequently in focus group discussions because of the dynamics of the discussion. For example, not all participants respond to each question, and the discussion can quickly shift direction to other topics because of comments offered by other participants. In addition, some topics can be mentioned once, briefly, by one person in a discussion, whereas other comments might be discussed by all participants and reiterated multiple times during the focus group.[21] In this way, the comments mentioned by the largest proportion of groups might not always reflect the topics that participants feel most strongly about or the views that everyone holds. Therefore, the order of frequency that we present in our figures should be viewed with caution. That said, we also include the proportion of groups in which someone expressed an opposing viewpoint. This helps determine whether there tends to be disagreement with certain views.

Fifth, as we discuss further later, the 1B4 career field has historically been cross-train-only, with personnel cross-training at different points in their careers. Because of this, it is possible that some of our more senior participants had been in the career field for a shorter period than some of the more junior participants. Although we did look at participant comments by grade to explore whether there were differences between more-senior and more-junior personnel, we did not split 1B4 participant comments out by length of time in the career field and therefore cannot tease out whether viewpoints by 1B4s differ notably by the number of years they have spent in the career field.

Finally, our exploration of the topic of recruiting and retention was intended as a quick look; we included it in our study because of the concerns expressed by some participants about those topics. It was not intended as a comprehensive study of those issues. For that reason, additional recommendations could be identified with additional research.

Organization of This Report

This volume provides an overview of our focus group findings on recruiting and retention by presenting three types of information.[22] We discuss results for recruiting in Chapter 2, followed

---

[21] Note that a topic mentioned briefly by one person could be a point with which everyone wholeheartedly agrees, and participants might choose not to add to it because they would just be repeating what the other participant has already said. In addition, a point that is discussed at length by participants might be discussed at length because the point is complicated and hard to explain, not because it is more important.

[22] As a reminder, Volume I focuses on the results related to training and development of the workforce. Volume II focuses on results related to recruiting and retention.

by results for retention in Chapter 3. We provide our recommendations in Chapter 4. Appendix A presents results separately for 1B4s, 1N4As, and CMF civilians, and Appendix B provides our questionnaire methodology.

2. Workforce Views on Recruiting

We explored views on recruiting and retention at the start of each focus group by asking cyber workforce participants whether they thought recruiting or retention was a concern for their specialty and why.[23] As shown in Figure 2.1, in every discussion, participants responded by either offering their thoughts on why recruiting was or was not a problem or directly stating that it was or was not a problem.[24] Views about why recruiting was or was not a problem were generated by participants organically (i.e., without prompting about a specific topic) and are shown in Figure 2.2.

Views on whether recruiting was a concern were mixed (see Figure 2.1). In slightly less than half of the discussions, at least one person said there were challenges in recruiting the right personnel for the job, and, in more than half of the discussions, someone suggested that there were no such challenges.[25]

When we asked participants why they thought recruiting was or was not a problem, they offered a variety of answers. Those that were raised in more than three groups (i.e., more than 10 percent of the discussions) are shown in Figure 2.1 and discussed in the sections that follow.

---

[23] Our discussion of training followed the discussion of recruiting and retention in each focus group or interview (see Volume I for the results of our training discussions).

[24] As a reminder, we present figures showing the overall results across all of the focus groups (with 1B4s, 1N4As, and civilians combined) throughout the main body of the report. In the text, we point out instances in which the responses were qualitatively different. For results for 1B4s, 1N4As, and civilians presented separately, see Appendix A.

[25] Note that the total of "yes" and "no" answers reported in response to this question can sum to more than 100 percent because more than one viewpoint can be expressed in a single focus group. In this case, in at least a few of the groups, both views were expressed.

Figure 2.1. Percentage of Focus Groups That Mentioned Specific Topics About Recruiting

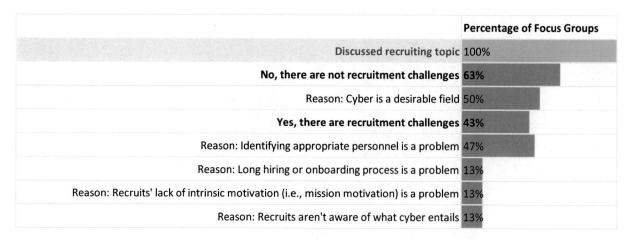

	Percentage of Focus Groups
Discussed recruiting topic	100%
No, there are not recruitment challenges	63%
Reason: Cyber is a desirable field	50%
Yes, there are recruitment challenges	43%
Reason: Identifying appropriate personnel is a problem	47%
Reason: Long hiring or onboarding process is a problem	13%
Reason: Recruits' lack of intrinsic motivation (i.e., mission motivation) is a problem	13%
Reason: Recruits aren't aware of what cyber entails	13%

NOTE: Percentages represent the number of focus groups in which a topic was mentioned by at least one person.

Why Recruiting Might Not Be a Concern: The Desirability of the Cyber Mission

In half of the discussions, participants noted that the cyber mission (specifically, the opportunity to hack into enemy networks or thwart an enemy's attacks on U.S. networks) is what draws personnel to the career field. This was the primary reason that participants offered for why they think recruiting in the offensive and defensive cyber specialties is not a concern.

> This is the career field of the future . . . to maintain and keep our data safe and to keep things running. [The adversary can] take away data and turn off the power; it can all be done with a computer. Being the ones to protect it or stop [the adversary] from being able to use theirs—that is the future. I don't think there is any problem finding people who want to be here. I have heard there are problems getting civilians in. Six months is a long time to get someone in the door, and other companies are paying really well to do this job. [1B4]

Participants described their career field as "cool," the "sexy career field," and even "the new hotness," and they discussed how it was viewed by many as one of the most desirable career fields for that reason.

> Within the Air Force, the 1B4 career field is viewed as an elitist type of career field. People come for the bragging rights, but they don't often know what they are getting into when they say, "Hey, I want to be a 1B." [1B4]

Many participants echoed these sentiments in their responses to the open-ended question on the questionnaire that asked what they like most about the career field. For example, about half mentioned that the mission is unique or that the work is impactful, and nearly 40 percent mentioned that the work is challenging or offers constant opportunities for learning. See Table 2.1 for examples of these write-in comments.

Table 2.1. Sample Questionnaire Write-In Responses to "What Do You Like the Most About Your Job?": The Mission and the Challenge

Category	Number of Mentions[a]	Responses
Unique mission; impact of work	33	• I also enjoy feeling like I am working on very pertinent issues that have a great effect on the world at large • Make a difference that has a significant real-world impact to a wide range of missions. • I get to see the impact of my efforts • Contribution to national defense, helping protect the country, directly observe effects • I also like having a purpose in thinking like the adversary to stop/prevent future attacks. • Direct impact on world events • Making an impact, looking back at my work and be able to say "I did that"
Challenging work; constant learning	25	• It pushes my way of thinking (thinking out of the box) • Constant challenges, the enthusiasm for meaningful work, and the opportunities to constantly learn. • Always learning new tools or programs, or the latest cyber news. • I love the constant need to challenge my understanding of IT and how that technology can be used by my airmen or against my airmen. • The opportunity to learn many, many things related to IT and cyber. • I also enjoy the challenge that cyber presents, most issues are the first of their kind, and require flexibility. • The cyber career field is very challenging and intellectually stimulating

NOTES: Responses reflect participants' write-in responses. Only spelling mistakes were fixed. Sample size reflects the number of participants who responded to the questionnaire item "What do you like the most about your job?"
[a] Out of 67 respondents.

As discussed in Chapter 1, some 1B4s also noted that the 1B4 career field is unique in that personnel have not traditionally been recruited at the point of accession. Instead, the overwhelming majority of cyber personnel were serving in other USAF career fields when they applied to or were recruited into cyber. At the time this study was conducted, only a few personnel had entered into the 1B4 career field at accession, and allowing entry at that point was a recent change.[26] 1B4s have historically been cross-trained from other career fields only. This movement from one career field to another is sometimes referred to as *lateral entry*.

Participants described lateral entry as offering an advantage for recruiting the right personnel in that USAF has more time to find and attract personnel with latent abilities, and personnel are able to get a more realistic sense of the demands of a cyber job. USAF has a chance to observe an individual's performance in another setting for some period of time before admitting that person to the cyber field. In fact, some participants noted that many people join USAF with the

---

[26] See Bui, 2019. Personnel can cross-train into cyber from any USAF career field, and current personnel do come from a wide variety of career field backgrounds. We did not explore whether certain career fields are more likely than others to cross-train into cyber.

specific goal of moving into the cyber field. Because they are not permitted into it on day one, they instead join a different career field and wait for the opportunity to switch.

> Most of the guys don't want to be in their previous career field[s], and this is an opportunity. Most 1B4s are here because they want to be, not because they were forced—a huge difference compared to other career fields. [1B4]

Challenges to Recruitment

Identifying the Right Personnel

The most frequently cited recruiting concern that came up during our discussions (mentioned in 47 percent of the groups) was that USAF did not have the ability to identify the right personnel to bring into the career field, including the ability to find and attract personnel who have the right abilities and interests and screen out those who do not.

> We attract people [who] want to be in this career field. . . . It's that being in the Air Force [might not be what people want]. There are a lot of people that I talked to who say they want to join the career field because they can make a lot of money on the outside. It's not a bad thing, but they just know nothing about computers. There has to be some sort of filter. [1B4]

Some participants noted that recruiting targets (or numbers) for cyber were being met without a problem but that the quality of personnel might be more of an issue. For example, one participant talked about how incoming personnel were not necessarily knowledgeable about or motivated to meet the rigors of the job.[27]

> The problem is, we are getting a lot of people that are just not interested in the job. . . . When I went through, we geeked out on this stuff; we went home and bought cheap laptops and just had fun with it, and it was part of what we were interested in. I get a lot of people with zero interest in being a 1N4A, especially when we put them in a position where they have a pretty intensive pipeline to become an EA [exploit analyst] and about a 50-percent first-time fail rate, and they are not going to make it. [1N4A]
>
> ***
>
> The Air Force focuses on numbers rather than quality. It may be that half of my 1B4s suck because of the process, but I don't have the mechanism to weed them out. Thus, on my 3D0 [Cyberspace Operations specialty] and 1B4s, if they are exquisitely trained, then they go to the commercial side to be paid more money. [SME]
>
> ***

---

[27] This issue of recruiting personnel who might not be knowledgeable about or motivated to meet the rigors of the career field is not unique to cyber; however, because cyber requires a high level of problem-solving, self-study, and continuous learning, the impacts of a lack of motivation might be especially pronounced.

> We don't always get the right people in, because our career field has bonuses and we offer special duty pay. There are definitely folks that are chasing the money rather than doing it for the interest in cyber. [1B4]

Participants talked about the need to find personnel who might have high potential but no experience or exposure to cyber and no idea that they would be good at it.

> We don't need to recruit cyber people. We need to train and keep people. Prior to going to cyber, I had zero interest in cyber—zero skill set, no programming, knew no [Microsoft] Excel. However, I successfully got through one of the hardest cyber schools the military has to offer. I am certified in one of the most difficult positions in the cyber world. [1N4A]
>
> ***
>
> [We try] to find the airmen or 18-year-olds that have the aptitude to perform in this domain. What are we doing to attract and recruit hackers? We don't recruit and attract; we build them. Because, out of high school, they don't have computer science degrees. On [the] enlisted side, it is a different beast. We may be able to find 18-year-olds who do not know a lot about cyber but have the cognition and aptitude to learn it. Try to map out cyber aptitude and cognition. We are trying to implement those as screeners and adjust screening tools. We are seeing some promise, but, right now, it is a manual process. [1B4]

Some participants also talked about barriers that prevent talented personnel or those with high potential from being able to enter the career field.

> So, people are interested, but they aren't able to get in, or, instead, uninterested people are getting in. I'd say it's 50-50. Fifty percent who get in are really cyber-focused and care. About 90 percent of those people will pass and go on to work. The other 10 percent will fail and go through CWO [Cyber Warfare Operations—Apprentice Course, initial skills training] or get alternative certification. [1B4]

In addition, a participant noted that congressional mandates to quickly field Cyber National Mission Force (CNMF) teams may have led in part to some quality problems among recruits, even if the number of recruits was meeting the demand.

> When I came through, there was a congressional mandate to have CNMF teams set up, so there was just a mad push. You had to get everyone that you could. . . . Hopefully, with that calming down, that will influence the career field. They can be a little pickier with who they're bringing in. [1B4]

As noted earlier, some participants viewed the lateral entry of 1B4s as a positive for recruiting. However, although lateral entry was viewed as a positive by some, others pointed out that it might prevent some talented personnel from joining in the first place. These personnel might not be willing to serve in a completely different occupation for some period of time, especially with no guarantee that they would ever get a chance to move into the job they really desired. Some participants also expressed the view that the internal process might still be excluding talented personnel and failing to identify those who have an aptitude for the job but no awareness that they would be good at it.

> I don't think there's a problem attracting the people. I think there's a problem getting the people. AFPC policy regarding retraining—it took me four tries to get into retraining. I kept getting denied, even though I could get through all the screening and everything. That was my biggest hurdle. [1B4]

Although the issue of recruiting the right personnel was frequently discussed in the focus groups, the questionnaire helps us understand how much of an issue respondents really think it is. In the questionnaire, we asked about satisfaction with the level of cyber talent being recruited and whether participants agreed that USAF is not attracting personnel with the right abilities.[28] As shown in Figure 2.2, on average, participants neither agreed nor disagreed that attracting personnel with the right abilities was a problem, and they were neither satisfied nor dissatisfied with the level of cyber talent. This suggests that the issue might not be dire, but the neutral rating also suggests that the quality of recruits is an issue that USAF has not adequately addressed. If it were adequately addressed (i.e., USAF was recruiting the best talent and attracting personnel with the right abilities), we would expect the responses to these items to be much more positive.

Figure 2.2. Average Responses to Questionnaire Items About the Quality of Personnel Being Recruited

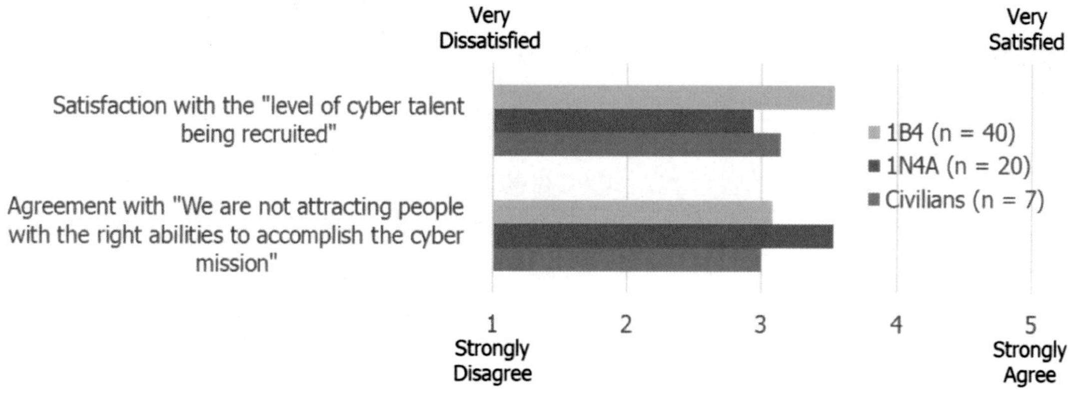

A Protracted Onboarding Process

Once a person is hired into the career field as a 1B4, 1N4A, or civilian, the onboarding process that allows that person to actually start working can, in many cases, take a significant amount of time. In 13 percent of the discussions, at least one participant said that this issue was having a meaningful impact on enthusiasm for their specialty. In the 1B4 and 1N4A cases, the onboarding process involves extensive training that can take more than two years to complete

---

[28] We did not directly explore what defines people with the right abilities in this study. However, we did explore it in our prior report about the cyber officer workforce (Hardison et al., 2019). The same general types of knowledge, skills, and abilities as those mentioned in Hardison et al., 2019, were mentioned in passing during our discussions in this study, including logical thinking, critical thinking, problem-solving, motivation for self-study, and past experience with cyber.

before new hires are allowed to begin working in the career field. For more on this, see Chapter 3.

For civilians, however, the major onboarding obstacles happen before personnel can even start training, and multiple participants expressed concern that this was likely leading to the loss of many exceptional candidates. Participants discussed two specific types of civilian onboarding problems.

One was that former airmen-turned-civilians have to wait 180 days after retirement before entering the career field.[29] Participants explained that, during this wait time, most people need some form of income to pay the bills and are not content to simply sit and wait. Those who find private-sector jobs might then be out of the job market by the time the 180 days are up.

> The big thing with civilians is that 180-day waiver. . . . If he's getting out and he's trained and I want to bring him in as a civilian, he's got to wait 180 days to do a waiver, and, by that time, we've hired someone else. If they got rid of that . . . I've seen so many folks that will qualify for civilian jobs go on [to], of course, better-paying contract jobs, when all they wanted to do was stay with the unit they were with [in] the Air Force. [Workforce—other[30]]

> ***

> I don't think there is any problem finding people who want to be here. I have heard there are problems getting civilians in. Six months is a long time to get someone in the door, and other companies are paying really well to do this job really well. [1B4]

This chilling effect of the 180-day wait period for recently retired personnel could pose a potential loss to USAF for two reasons. First, the best and the brightest are the ones who are most likely to find work quickly during that 180 days and command the best jobs and the best salaries. The added pay and attractiveness of private-sector jobs might make it especially difficult for USAF to win back the best and brightest personnel when the 180-day wait period is up. Second, these just-retired USAF personnel who come from a military cyber career field are already trained and experienced in the mission. The loss of these individuals means the loss of a significant training investment on the part of USAF (two years of training), as well as the loss of personnel who are already deeply entrenched and experienced in the mission itself.

For those civilian applicants who do not have prior service or those who separate prior to retirement eligibility, there are obstacles that affect the success of the civilian hiring process. Some participants mentioned the impact of bureaucracy and various forms of red tape.

---

[29] The 180-day rule, which restricts DoD from hiring retired military personnel to civilian positions within the first six months of retirement, has been in place since 1964 but was waived when a state of national emergency was declared in September 2001. It was reinstated in the National Defense Authorization Act for Fiscal Year 2017, which took effect on December 23, 2016 (Salomon, 2017).

[30] *Other* encompasses anyone not in the 1B4, 1N4A, or civilian category.

The hiring process is very long, and, by the end, the person of interest is already receiving two or three other offers. [SME]

Other participants talked about how obtaining needed security clearances is one obstacle, in particular, that can lead to extreme time delays in a person's ability to start the job and ultimately start earning a paycheck.

I cannot bring anyone on, because we are a special, sensitive category; they have to have TS/SCI [Top Secret/Sensitive Compartmentalized Information] clearance. AFPC and the archaic process says we cannot ask about clearance in the interview process.[31] We have instances where we hire someone, and they don't have clearance, so we have to hold that position while we wait and see if they get clearance. They don't start until the clearance is in hand. We have a contractor right now who is willing to wait that out, so that position will be vacant. Other people say, "No, I will go find something else." That's the conundrum with hiring civilians. [SME]

Applicant Motivation

Another topic, which was mentioned in 13 percent of our discussions, relates to a lack of intrinsic motivation among some personnel who are attracted to the career field. Participants described two types of motivation issues. The first is the importance of being a self-starter and being motivated to learn new content on one's own and during one's free time. Participants explained that this is an issue for recruiting in that the career field might not be doing the best job of weeding out personnel who do not have a self-starter mentality. The other motivation issue is that some personnel enter the career field with the intention of getting as many certifications and as much training as possible and leaving the service as soon as possible for a lucrative career in the private sector. Participants explained that they wished that they could do a better job of screening out personnel who do not have the interests of USAF's mission at heart.

Recruits Not Being Aware of What Cyber Entails

How well USAF recruiters are able to market the various career fields makes a difference, and this issue was mentioned in 13 percent of the discussions. This seems to be of particular concern for the 1N4As; participants explained that it was difficult for recruiters to attract suitable personnel to the 1N4A career field because—given that so much of it (including the Career Field Education and Training Plan) is classified—they have little to no information to provide on job parameters and skill set expectations. Recruiters also might be entirely unfamiliar with the job themselves, again because the information is classified.

Whenever I came to join, I did not know what this job was. I think clarification on what the job does would help with attracting [people]. I think the Air Force

---

[31] Although AFPC might be the organization responsible for executing various clearance rules and regulations regarding when in the hiring process the security clearance processes can start, federal regulations for hiring civilians might be guiding some of these policies.

has an issue explaining what cyber is. The recruiters could be more knowledgeable about what our roles are. When I joined, the recruiter said I would be hacking stuff. And I said, "That sounds cool, so sign me up." That's all they could tell me. [1N4A]

***

I've spoken with very few individuals who actually knew what this job was coming into it. There were a few in JCAC [Joint Cyber Analysis Course] who had computer science degrees, and it was something they were very suited for and where they wanted to be. Most folks, the recruiters weren't able to inform enough about the job. They have like a paragraph on like About.com, but it doesn't really tell you what the person will be doing. So, when I came in, I had no idea what this job would really entail outside of the name. [SME]

***

The recruiters don't know what 1N4A is. As far as I know, no 1N4A have become recruiters, so the knowledge is not spread to the recruiter career field. [SME]

In addition, as shown in Figure 2.1, it was clear from discussions that some participants felt that the public or other USAF personnel might not be aware of USAF's cyber mission. This would, therefore, affect who applies for the job in ways that have nothing to do with a recruiter. They explained that this general lack of awareness could prevent some personnel who might be a great addition to the career field from being identified and recruited. This is a problem that could be occurring in both of the enlisted specialties, as well as in the civilian ones.

3. Workforce Views on Retention and Data on Past Retention

In this chapter, we discuss participants' views on what might drive retention within the community and whether participants see reasons for concern about retention. We include both focus group participants' comments from our discussions and their responses to the related questionnaire items. At the end of this chapter, we briefly explore whether historical USAF personnel data support the conclusion that retention might be a concern within the enlisted workforce.

Participant Views on Retention

When we started our conversation with participants, we told them that we were interested in talking about both recruiting and retention issues in the focus groups. In many of our discussions, participants started by talking about recruiting issues, but then they quickly contrasted recruiting with retention, saying that recruiting is not what they are really concerned about, but retention is. According to one participant, "Recruiting, we do a great job . . . but we can't keep them happy." This view that retention is a concern was echoed in the overwhelming majority of discussions (77 percent), as shown in Figure 3.1.

In the handful of groups in which participants said the opposite—specifically, that retention is not a problem—they also offered the following explanations:

> On the military side, I don't think we have a retention problem compared to the rest of the Air Force. There are many reasons for that. One is quality missions, putting us on quality missions versus missions that prepare for inspection. Our missions are getting better, but we still have a lot of improvement for getting better. Air Force pays them special duty assignment pay. That helps. They also get a real nice reenlistment bonus that helps out also. [Workforce—other]

> ***

> There are multiple reasons that motivate people to stay. [For] some people, it is about hope. Some people like to serve more than anything else, because the military is very structured, and they like it. Some hope that they will eventually get to do the job—they will do great no matter what, and money isn't a factor. For some people, the market is not where they want it to be—they could be in an area where, if they got out, it may not be as beneficial money-wise. [1B4]

> ***

> A lot of that is attributed to them enjoying what they do, and being technical on the keyboards, and going after the bad guys, and also special duty assignment pay and reenlisted bonuses. [Workforce—other]

Those participants who did express concerns about retention offered a variety of reasons. They raised those reasons without us prompting them about a particular topic, in response to the question: "Why do you think retention is an issue?" The reasons that were raised in more than three groups (more than 10 percent of the discussions) are shown in Figure 3.1. We discuss each in the sections that follow.

Figure 3.1. Percentage of Focus Groups That Mentioned Specific Issues About Retention

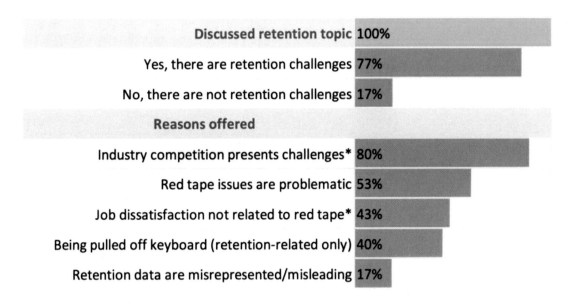

NOTE: Sometimes, an issue was raised by one person, and an opposite view was expressed by someone in the same discussion group. In those cases, the same discussion would be counted in both the issue frequency and the opposite sentiment frequency. For some topics, no opposite sentiment was expressed in the workforce discussions. When an opposite sentiment was expressed in more than 7 percent of the workforce discussions, it was added to the figure. Where an opposite sentiment was expressed in 3 to 7 percent of the workforce focus groups (i.e., one or two groups), the category is marked with an asterisk. Percentages represent the number of focus groups in which an issue was mentioned by at least one person.

Competition from Industry

Regarding retention, the most common topic mentioned across our focus groups (in 80 percent of them) pertained to the allure of private-sector cyber jobs that pay well and are less bureaucratic in nature than military jobs. Some participants described instances in which personnel cross-trained for the sole purpose of getting the requisite experience and moving on to the private sector. So, it is possible that some personnel might plan from the outset for their USAF cyber careers to be a short-lived preparatory step for something "larger" or more lucrative.

> Overall, a lot of people come in, get their training, and go out and get a much higher paying job on the outside. [We need to] try to keep those individuals in the Air Force. [1B4]
>
> ***
>
> Every day, I hire folks, and, the next day, I get someone that says, "I'm moving on." We are hiring folks as GS-11s and 12s, and they are there for maybe a year or so, pad their resume a little more, and they are gone. It's just hard to compete,

and I don't know how to fix that at this point other than pay more or make this an environment where it's easier to entice folks to stay. [Workforce—other]

***

I believe there are two parts to the retention problem among cyber personnel. The first part is driven by money. Some individuals have joined the military to do their time and get out. For them, I believe that money is [the] driving force behind their decision[s] to leave. People come into the 1B4 career field, do their four-ish years, get training and operational experience, and then are offered a $100K-per-year job easily. The second part of this is poor leadership, connection to leadership, or sense of camaraderie. For the people that fall into this second group, I believe they joined with the intention of staying in and supporting their country but have been burned out by poor leadership and lack of interest in the nontechnical side. [1B4]

***

I think it will always be difficult to retain people who can look across the line and say, "Hey, I can do this same thing for more money and not have to wear a uniform. Or run. Those aren't going to be requirements. Or deploy." As long as the Air Force has to have certain requirements on the table and is limited by how much money they can pay people, it'll be difficult to retain those individuals. I think you will retain the people who actually care about the mission and want to serve and will serve whether they're doing a cool, snazzy job or not. But you are not going to retain the best and brightest when they can make a ton of money on the outside. I think that's a lost objective. [1B4]

In one or two groups, participants offered an opposite viewpoint about concerns that personnel might be leaving USAF for industry, citing the advantages of staying in and the importance of the USAF cyber mission. For example, a 1B4 interviewee, when asked about retention and what he liked most about his job, replied, "Doing stuff that I can't do anyplace else. The community—this has been the best squadron I've ever been a part of, it's a very close-knit community, and we take care of each other." Someone else noted that the draw of the pay in the civilian market was not necessarily the deciding factor for some personnel:

> You can make more on the outside typically, but then all that is taxable. As Air Force, half of my income isn't taxable, and the benefits of being able to retire . . . the extra benefits of base access, flying on hops, medical benefits, and bonuses definitely help too. [1B4]

Red Tape and Bureaucratic Issues

In 53 percent of our focus groups, participants pointed to hassles related to "red tape" and bureaucracy as driving personnel loss, and some described the private sector as an easy escape. There was no single definition offered for this variety of challenges; rather, participants tended to classify such tasks as wearing a uniform, writing reports, training for and taking physical fitness tests, and attending commander's calls as *red tape*—tasks that one 1B4 labeled "unnecessarily mandatory." Likewise, a 1N4A added, "We go through all this training, and 90 percent of what we do is cutting through red tape." These bureaucratic issues were described as hamstringing personnel across the career fields, to include civilians and the protracted hiring process that they must endure before contributing to the cyber mission. One participant offered civilian security clearance delays as an example:

> It is stupid things like security clearances. [We] cannot send civilians through [the Cyber] 300 [course] because half require top-level security clearance and [we] cannot send them to the course. [SME]

Participants talked at length about the allure of not having to contend with the myriad of additional duties, red tape, and other pressures that exist in USAF, which leads personnel to consider private-sector options. In most cases, participants also noted that the pay differential makes the red tape, bureaucracy, and additional duties especially hard to tolerate.

> You will see a lot of people who have been a 1B4 for years, and, next thing, they are tired of the military, the red tape, not being able to do something to help the mission because someone higher up doesn't understand what the experts down below are talking about. And then they hear about the civilian, their friend, saying, "Hey, yeah, I got out, and now I am making six figures, and I am the lead engineer or technician of this workshop, and I have the freedom to do what I need to do." [1B4]
>
> ***
>
> A staff sergeant I knew had all of these ideas about how to make things better. He was met by level after level of bureaucracy and red tape, and he ended up leaving to get an outside job paying $160K. [1B4]
>
> ***
>
> Some say the Air Force is very bureaucratic. They need something and have to wait for months to get it. On the enlisted side, they don't have to worry about deployment or doing additional duties if they go into the private sector. They have to worry about so much on the enlisted side right now. [1B4]
>
> ***
>
> I feel like there is a lot of bureaucratic red tape involved, that we operate with our hands behind our backs so often. I have friends who got out, and they say, "I actually get to just go to work and do my job, and that feels great." [1B4]
>
> ***
>
> The bureaucracy associated with the government military is completely the opposite of how a lot of these guys operate. They want to go do things, to do the job, not go through 50 levels of red tape to maybe be able to do the job. I think that is more on the retention side because they get in and . . . find themselves unable to do what they thought they were going to do. [1N4A]

Red tape was also one of the more frequently mentioned topics in the questionnaire write-in responses. See Table 3.1 for examples.

Table 3.1. Sample Questionnaire Write-In Responses to "What Do You Like the Least About Your Job?": Red Tape and Policy Issues

Category	Number of Mentions[a]	Responses
Red tape and policy-related issues or changes	14	• The pointless bureaucracy that takes precedent over actual mission accomplishment • The bureaucratic and political workplace overhead that leads to burnout and slowing in the advancement of infosec [information security] capability • Constant organizational changes • Endless checklists • Bureaucratic barrier inhibits the tactical level day to day • Enormous bureaucracy with defensive weapon system improvements • Policies keep us from doing the job we were trained to do

NOTES: Responses reflect participants' write-in responses. Only spelling mistakes were fixed. Sample size reflects the number of participants who responded to the questionnaire item "What do you like the least about your job?"
[a] Out of 64 respondents.

Wanting to Remain "On Keyboard"

In addition to the allure of industry, participants in 40 percent of our focus groups said that personnel leave the career field because they are unhappy about being "pulled off keyboard." They felt stymied from doing what they were most passionate about—i.e., conducting OCO or DCO. Those drawing a straight line between retention and remaining on keyboard often pointed to the pressure to promote and assume more administrative or leadership responsibilities, both of which equate to less time performing the more technical aspects of their jobs. As one 1N4A put it, "Most people join this career field because they enjoy the technical aspect, not because they want to be administrators." Another illustrated this idea through a fictitious character:

> For a majority of them, it's not about making [thousands more in pay]; it's more about living the lifestyle that "Tim" lives as opposed to a senior master sergeant lives. Tim rolls in at 8:00 a.m. with his pajamas on. Everyone loves Tim. Tim leaves on time, and, the truth is, if you do well and you promote in the Air Force, eventually in ten to 15 years you are no longer hands on keyboard; you are told you shouldn't be. Those are some serious retention issues when it comes to, "Wow, I want to do this for my career, for longer than ten years, and I don't want to have to deal with writing EPRs [enlisted performance reports]." [1N4A]

Although some 1N4As offered comments about wanting to remain on keyboard (such as those above), the majority of perspectives came from 1B4s.

> I've been a computer nerd since the 1980s. I love electronics; I love computers. I understand these kinds of people; they don't want to be bogged down with something that isn't fun to them. Admin[istrative work] isn't fun. You are going to pull me off of this mission because you want to put me up for an award. Some people like that, but I would rather stay on keyboard and figure out the problem in front of me. Personally, I don't care about awards. [1B4]

***

My previous supervisor was in [intelligence]—he was one of the last in intel to be doing cyber [operations] side. He got out because intel was going to pull him back and he didn't want to do leadership—he wanted to stay technical. They said, "We want to pull you off keyboard," and he said no and separated. [1B4]

***

The rank of technical sergeant is the last rank you can get where you're still hands on keyboard. I would say most people in cyber are wanting to do the hands-on-keyboard stuff. On the officer side, it's up until major that you can do tech, then you get shipped off to do more leadership stuff. [1B4]

***

In the military, if you stay in and get promoted, you're going to gravitate away from that outstanding typist over there. You're going to gravitate away from that keyboard, and you'll be writing performance reports, you're going to be writing appraisals. You're going to be attending meetings. You're going to be doing more leadership things. We're failing in two ways. One, we're not developing leaders; we're developing technicians. I have failed as a squadron commander, and we are failing as an Air Force in the cyber workforce. I see a lot of our junior officers and senior NCOs [noncommissioned officers] and they just suck at leading. They suck at managing, but they are awesome at that keyboard. [SME]

Table 3.2 provides similar examples from the questionnaire.

Table 3.2. Sample Questionnaire Write-In Responses to "What Do You Like the Least About Your Job?": Being Pulled Off Keyboard

Category	Number of Mentions[a]	Responses
Being pulled off keyboard	8	• Having to perform duties outside of my AFSC [Air Force specialty code]; i.e., additional duties • I feel like I have two full time jobs and it can get very stressful at times. I have my operational side and my admin side. • Additional duties that keep me from performing my job • I dislike how the new members get stuck doing work that detracts from their training • E-7 and above typically get vectored towards administrative tasks

NOTES: Responses reflect participants' write-in responses. Only spelling mistakes were fixed. Sample size reflects the number of participants who responded to the questionnaire item "What do you like the least about your job?"
[a] Out of 64 respondents.

Misutilization of Personnel

In Volume I of this report, we discussed at length participants' perceptions of the misutilization of personnel who have in-depth specialized training. When we asked about training issues and concerns, the general topic of misutilization of personnel came up in 43 percent of the discussions (see Harding et al., 2021).

However, this issue also came up as a potential driver of personnel loss, so we present the same results in this volume. Participants explained that personnel felt discouraged when they felt that their training and skill sets were not being appropriately utilized. Participants also explained that personnel generally believed that their specialized training, skills, and expertise would be much better utilized in private-sector organizations. This perceived misutilization of personnel in USAF was leading some personnel to want to leave the military.

As shown in Figure 3.2, overall, participants reported that their skills and training were not being well utilized. IB4s responded with only slight agreement on average when asked whether their skills were utilized well in their unit and their talents were used well in the workplace. More specifically, the mean response was close to halfway between a 3 (neither agree nor disagree) and a 4 (somewhat agree). This suggests that 1B4s think that there is still considerable room for improvement in the utilization of their skills. Civilians tended to be a little more positive than 1B4s. In contrast, on these same questions, 1N4As tended to be slightly dissatisfied with how personnel are utilized.

As a potential solution, some participants suggested that USAF devise a better talent-management system for 1B4s, providing personnel with more-relevant work assignments, putting more effort into assigning personnel to work roles depending on which skills they need to develop, rotating personnel more often, and defining work roles more clearly.

Figure 3.2. Average Responses to Questions About Utilization of Talent

As shown in Table 3.3, the fact that utilization of personnel could be an important driver of retention is further supported by the write-in comments in response to the question about what participants liked the least about their jobs. In response to that question, several participants noted that the role of cyber personnel in USAF was not clear and that their training and experience were not being utilized properly.

Table 3.3. Sample Questionnaire Write-In Responses to "What Do You Like the Least About Your Job?": Unclear Role or Misutilization

Category	Number of Mentions[a]	Responses
Unclear roles for cyber personnel; unclear role of cyber in the USAF mission, cyber personnel misutilized	15	• Lack of utilization of training in the workplace • Lack of long-term thinking when applied to the individual and what training/experience they have • How we manage (or fail to manage) our talent • The confusion of what operator roles entail • The lack of direction as to where and how to use cyber protection teams • The apparent lack of understanding from higher level leadership of our capabilities • Unclear operational vision • There is no single, clear, and concise understanding of what is expected of a 1N4A • Leadership does not necessarily understand the proper role of cyber in digital environment

NOTES: Responses reflect participants' write-in responses. Only spelling mistakes were fixed. Sample size reflects the number of participants who responded to the questionnaire item "What do you like the least about your job?"
[a] Out of 64 respondents.

Other Areas of Satisfaction and Dissatisfaction Related to Retention

In addition, in 43 percent of our discussions, participants described other sources of dissatisfaction not directly captured in the previous categories. Some of these comments reflected entirely distinct ideas from the other categories, while some related to the previously discussed categories but did not explicitly or directly articulate the point in a way that allowed us to definitively code it into the previously discussed categories. For example, when someone says that a person left because they were "frustrated because they do not get to do the things they want to do," it could mean that they were frustrated with not being able to stay on keyboard, with dealing with red tape, or with both. The following are additional examples:

> It's not just the pay; it's the "Why is this person always in my chili when I'm just trying to do my work?" [Workforce—other]
>
> ***
>
> I think it is difficult to keep the right people. The people who are really skilled and have a desire to do this job leave because they are frustrated because they do not get to do the things they want to do. [1N4A]
>
> ***
>
> When you get training to do a lot of different things, you have a hunger to do it and to grow in it, and the military sometimes limits you to do something. I think some people want to do more or use their skill set more. [1N4A]
>
> ***

> Unlike the other services, our cyber forces are broken up into 1B4 (operators) and 1N4A (analysts). The rest of the service is not like this; everything falls into the same career field. They thought they had the ability to become an operator, and that wasn't actually true. [1N4A]

Several comments were made by focus group participants that reflected dissatisfaction related to pay equity. In particular, enlisted airmen felt that it was unfair that they were paid substantially less than civilians or officers who occupied similar roles.

> My officer counterpart does the exact same thing that I do and makes twice as much. It's annoying. [1B4]

> ***

> I've worked with civilians that I know I'm better than, and they make double [what] I do. [1N4A]

In addition, some participants discussed the idea of a merger between 1N4As and 1B4s as being a good idea, while others expressed reservations about it. This was one training-related policy change that was being debated by leadership at the time of our discussions;[32] however, no final answer regarding whether the merger would take place had been made at that time. See Appendix C of Volume I for examples of the pros and cons of such a merger offered by participants.

Write-in comments on the questionnaire also provide insights into other possible drivers of attraction to and retention in the career field that include and go beyond those discussed in the previous sections. Those are summarized in Tables 3.4 and 3.5.

Primary sources of satisfaction (shown in Table 3.4) include training opportunities, the technical aspects of the job, and enjoyment garnered from working with others in the career field. Other unique sources of satisfaction include the high degree of job autonomy and influence on decisionmaking, commercial training options, and working in the joint environment. Notably, a few participants mentioned career opportunities (two of these comments were specifically related to postmilitary employment), and two participants discussed only negative aspects of their career in response to being asked about what they liked most about their jobs.

Primary additional sources of dissatisfaction (shown in Table 3.5) included lack of training options and practice environments and lack of support and guidance from leadership. Other commonly mentioned sources of dissatisfaction included pay and the lack of impact on the mission. A few participants mentioned other aspects of their jobs, such as environmental pressures, inability to become experts in their careers, having multiple bosses, lack of promotion opportunities, and the selection of cyber personnel.

---

[32] The merger was being considered because of the considerable overlap in training, skills, and work that exists between the two career fields. The merger was discussed in the context of potential changes to training and, therefore, we included this topic in Volume I. However, the merger also has implications for recruiting and retention to the extent that it could affect job satisfaction in one or both of the career fields, either positively or negatively.

Table 3.4. Sample Questionnaire Write-In Responses to "What Do You Like the Most About Your Job?": Other Sources of Satisfaction

Category	Number of Mentions[a]	Responses
Training opportunities	20	• Cyber is a new field and we are getting trained, getting work experience • The ability and time during work hours to do advanced training (when funds are available) • The amount of training to augment said experience is also great. • Almost all of our training is challenging and mentally stimulating, and I am learning things I would never learn anywhere else.
Technical aspects	18	• The interaction with new technology • I enjoy working with computers at this skill level. • The hands-on analysis and technicality mixed with the need for critical thinking keeps it lively and fresh. • Working with large scale networks—challenges us technically • My passion is in computers and technology
Coworker satisfaction	11	• I am surrounded by the most intelligent airmen that I have ever served with. • I'm surrounded by intelligent thought-provoking people • Working as a team with a highly skilled group of professionals who are committed • The personnel that I have worked with in the community are some of the most intelligent and professional people I have ever met. • The ability to be associated with like-minded professionals (same interests).
Job perks and qualities	10	• The good work/life balance in my current assignment • I enjoy the travel • The consistent schedule, special duty assignment pay, reenlistment bonuses
Autonomy and influence on decisions	9	• The autonomy to make decisions and execute missions as I determine • The community is also, in general, very open to different ideas and always willing to engage in discussion about anything. • The ability to influence how low-level tasks are executed • Ability to influence the future of cyber. • I enjoy the possible scope of influence I can have when conducting mission
Career opportunities	7	• Variety/"directions" you can go with your technical career; set up for civilian employment • The ability to move on to another mission within cyber • Opportunity for growth, impact, advancement • A good baseline for postmilitary employment
Non-USAF training	3	• Training (commercial/joint) • I like the opportunities for commercial training
Joint partnership	2	• We are joint and working with mission partners • The joint environment

NOTES: Responses reflect participants' write-in responses. Only spelling mistakes were fixed. Sample size reflects the number of participants who responded to the questionnaire item "What do you like the most about your job?"
[a] Out of 64 respondents.

Table 3.5. Sample Questionnaire Write-In Responses to "What Do You Like the Least About Your Job?": Other Sources of Dissatisfaction

Category	Number of Mentions	Responses
Lack of or irrelevant training; lack of practice environment	16	• How we are tasked and expected to operate on mission without specific targeted intelligence • We are not trained properly • Unpolished/streamlined training that isn't relevant to the job • No formal planning courses, yet 1B4s become planners • The amount of time wasted waiting on training mission, etc. • Many times, there is no mission specific training • Air Force training (AETC) • Low training standards • Training—a lot of redundant time spent on the same material
Lack of leadership support, quality, and guidance; lack of trust in the workforce	13	• There are things that would highly benefit our mission but there are times we cannot do it due to leadership who don't trust the experts • Lack of understanding from leadership • The lack of clear leadership in all levels of our chain of command • Poor guidance lacking technical understanding • The inability for leaders to accept risk and empower the workforce • Trying to get older leaders to change perspective on cyber • Leadership does not know cyber • Lack of feedback • Having a civilian chain of command that does not understand the additional duties of active duty personnel
Dissatisfaction with pay or other job perk	9	• The reserves take 6+ months to pay for TDY [temporary duty] travel which puts significant strain on the member • My salary • Lack of assignment locations • Pay gap • I do the same job as an officer getting paid half the amount just because they have a degree which in cyber does not mean much
Lack of impact on mission or lack of vision about mission	7	• Not having visibility on whether our efforts on missions have any impact on how the Air Force/DoD utilizes cyber resources • We are given taskings that have little impact • Confusion, no knowledge of where things are going in the future • Lack of transparency of what was accomplished • The lack of mission
Environmental pressures and constraints	6	• Pressure, time, uptight environments because of classification we work in • Fear tie[s] the hands of 1B4s preventing innovation and efficiency • Everything is chaos. Everything is a fire that needs to be put out yesterday • Go the 8+ hours of sitting in a chair with minimal exposure to the outside world makes some people stir crazy
Problems with manning numbers	5	• The thought that we can be mass produced • 2–3 competing work roles at once—not enough people • The limited spaces for how many people there are in this career
Inability to become experts	5	• I dislike that we have to PCS [permanent change of station, meaning move from one assignment to the next] and/or change jobs before we get a chance to become TRUE subject-matter experts in our jobs.

Category	Number of Mentions	Responses
		• Rank structure too rigid to allow for proper skill development in highly technical field • Not possible to be 100 percent SMEs in all areas—host/network etc.
Multiple bosses	5	• The world we work in results in many bosses, which means many policies and conflicting information/desires. • Multiple bosses—NSA [National Security Agency], CYBERCOM [U.S. Cyber Command], USAF • Too many bosses, can never please everyone
Training does not evolve with cyber	4	• Integration of new capabilities is slow • It feels as though changes take more time to implement than to actual benefit from their effects • Lack of Air Force evolution in the career field • Air Force unable to adapt in adequate time for advancing technology
Lack of promotion or advancement	3	• Lack of technical advancement past GS-13 • Lack of promotion
Training timeline	3	• The gaps in time between training milestones which contribute to degradation of skills • The amount of time wasted waiting on training mission, etc. • Very long training pipeline
Retention of cyber personnel	2	• A lot of the best operators get out because the money in the private sector is so good. Wish we could do more to retrain our best • Leadership pretending there is not a retention problem
Selection of personnel	2	• I think the Air Force could do better at getting people who want to do this stuff, especially since it's skilled people they want. • Very little talent management
Other negative aspects of job[a]	2	• I have been consistently in positions that do not use my knowledge or training. I am a "leader" who does no cyber. • I liked the idea that I would be conducting cyber operations, however that wasn't the case

NOTES: Responses reflect participants' write-in responses. Only spelling mistakes were fixed. Some responses have been sorted into more than one category. The sample size for this question is 64 because three of the participants (out of 67 total questionnaire participants) did not respond to this item.
[a] These comments were given in response to the question "What you like the most about your job?" However, because they reflect dislikes about the job, we included them in this table.

How Concerned Are Participants About Retention?

In the previous sections, we covered the qualitative comments offered by participants in our discussions. In this section, we present data from the questionnaire that we gave these same participants. The data allow us to put participants' focus group comments in context by examining the *level* of concern that participants have about some of the topics they raised. For each questionnaire item, we display results for 1B4s, 1N4As, and civilians separately to allow for comparison by specialty, but it is important to note that the sample size for civilians is small ($n = 7$) relative to the other two groups, which means that any differences between civilian and enlisted views might be due to chance alone and, therefore, should be interpreted with caution.

As shown in Figure 3.3, the questionnaire suggests that the participants are, on average, dissatisfied with retention in their career field, and this sentiment was consistent across all three types of participants. The figure also shows that the enlisted participants responded fairly neutrally about whether they would be likely to stay on active duty if given the chance to leave. In addition, participants reported that they would have no trouble finding a job if they left, which is consistent with the comments offered about competition from industry. Taken as a whole, these results present a picture that suggests that retention issues (even if not present now) could possibly manifest quickly if personnel grow to be sufficiently dissatisfied in their USAF career fields.

Figure 3.3. Average Views on Retention from the Questionnaire

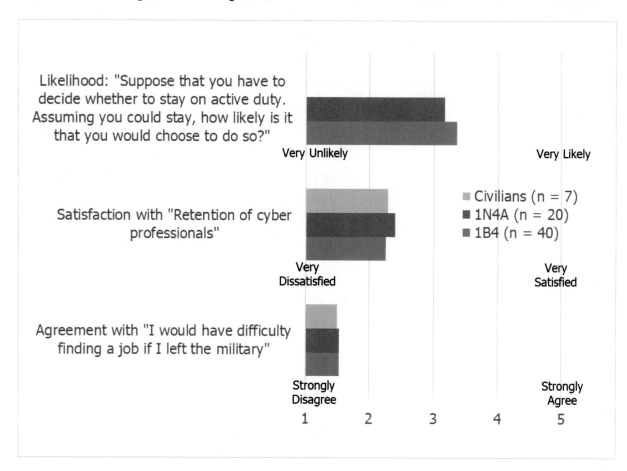

NOTE: Civilians were not asked about the likelihood that they would stay on active duty.

Participants from the 1N4A career field responded neutrally to several of the overall job satisfaction items, while civilian and 1B4 participants tended to respond more positively, as shown in Figure 3.4. This suggests that the 1N4A career field might be more at risk of retention issues than the other two groups, but, again, it is important to note that the sample size for each of the three groups is small relative to the sizes of the overall career fields and that the participants might not necessarily be representative of their entire career fields or specialties. As shown in Figure 3.5, 1B4s and civilians also responded slightly positively on average regarding satisfaction with their USAF careers in general and their current duty assignments; their views were more neutral on opportunities for promotions and special duty assignments. 1N4As again tended to have slightly lower means on these items overall, and their average responses were more neutral and, for some items, even negative (expressing mild dissatisfaction). This shows that, at least among our participants, there is room to raise satisfaction levels in these areas.

Some of the items that we included on the questionnaire are identical to or closely aligned with items on other surveys (e.g., the Federal Employee Viewpoint Survey, USAF retention surveys, and USAF climate surveys). We included them on our survey so that USAF could compare the views that were offered in our study with views that they might have collected on similar or identical items on other surveys of a larger sample of the same workforce. That comparison can allow USAF to better understand whether our participants are expressing views that are similar or distinctly different from those of the broader workforce.

One additional point worth noting about these satisfaction results is that they show that our qualitative findings (i.e., the comments and criticisms offered in the previous sections) do not simply reflect views of personnel who are disgruntled and unhappy about their jobs. They instead reflect views of participants who are at a minimum neither satisfied nor dissatisfied on average and in some cases are fairly positive about their jobs.

Figure 3.4. Average Job Satisfaction Ratings

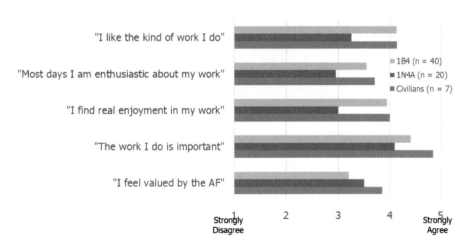

NOTE: AF = Air Force.

Figure 3.5. Average Satisfaction with Specific Aspects of the Job

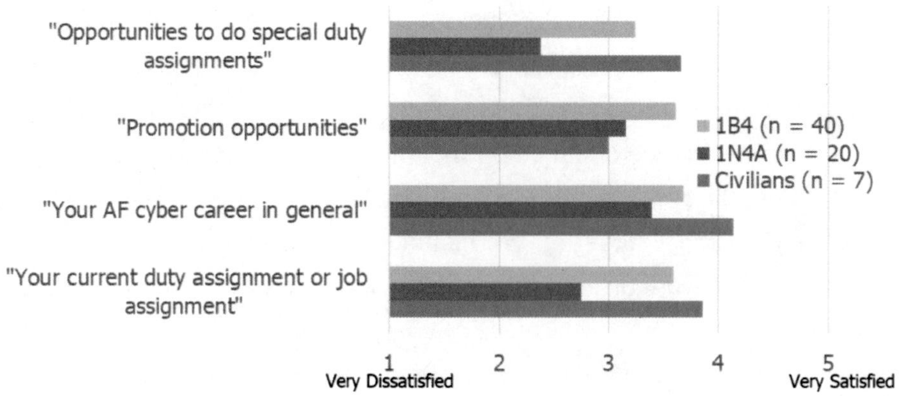

NOTE: AF = Air Force.

Do Personnel Data Support the Conclusion That There Is a Retention Problem?

USAF personnel data, as shown in Figure 3.6, suggest that retention numbers for the enlisted career fields are not necessarily a problem relative to the overall retention numbers observed across USAF. With this fact in mind, however, some participants noted that a look at overall retention numbers might be misleading (this came up in 17 percent of our discussions, as shown in Figure 3.1). They explained that the number of personnel retained might be fine, but the quality of those leaving is concerning. Participants pointed to this loss of quality in a variety of ways, saying that the career fields are "bleeding talent," that "every good operator is leaving," and that only the "mediocre people" are staying.

To explore this issue further, we looked at whether personnel who have higher Armed Forces Qualification Test (AFQT) scores are more likely to leave.[33] First, we split the retention data into AFQT quartile groups. That is, we looked at the entire sample of 1B4s and their AFQT scores and set the quartile boundaries based on that entire range. The bottom 25 percent of AFQT scores in the 1B4 set the boundary for the lower quartile, the next 25 percent of scores set the

---

[33] Ideally, a direct measure of cyber performance on the job would be used to distinguish exceptional performers in the retention data; however, there are currently no clear ways to identify top cyber performers in the personnel data files. In the absence of such a measure, we turned to AFQT scores as a proxy. AFQT scores are composite scores created from the Armed Services Vocational Aptitude Battery, which is used for screening recruits and qualifying them for certain jobs. AFQT is generally thought of as an assessment of an individual's overall cognitive ability or aptitude. In other words, we are assuming that the people with the highest overall aptitude scores are likely to be those who show excellence in cyber performance on the job. Cognitive ability has been consistently shown to be a strong predictor of training performance and job performance across all types of jobs, and the strength of these relationships is greater as job complexity and training complexity increase (see, for example, Schmidt and Hunter, 1998). We therefore think that this is a reasonable way of identifying personnel who are likely to be among the top cyber performers and that it is therefore a reasonable proxy for performance. However, as noted, we also acknowledge that having the ability to directly identify top performers would be ideal.

next boundary, and so on. Then, we plotted the data to see whether retention lines diverged. We also did this for the 1N4As, and the results for both are shown in Figure 3.7. The figure shows that personnel in the top quartiles appear to be leaving at higher rates at certain points in their careers.

With respect to the 1B4 data, it is important to note that the first few years of data (through year 6) have some small sample sizes because the point of cross flow happens later in some personnel's careers than in others' careers. However, between years 7 and 14, the sample sizes range from the low 20s to the 30s and even 40s in some cases. As a result, the observed differences in retention rates are more stable, and we see a dip in retention of personnel in the upper quartiles in those years relative to one or both of the lower quartiles. For 1N4As, the sample sizes are also sufficiently large in the earlier years. Overall, these figures suggest that the personnel with the highest aptitudes might in fact be leaving at higher rates than others in the career field, which is consistent with our participants' concerns.

One additional point worth noting about the 1B4 retention figures is that, because the career field has historically been cross-train-only, the retention data that we present in these figures are based entirely on cross-train-only personnel. However, because of the 2019 change from a cross-train-only career field to one that now recruits potential personnel at enlistment, we know that the retention profiles for the career field will look very different in the coming years as more and more personnel start their 1B4 careers in their first year of service. How this will affect retention in the career field going forward is still unknown. The 1N4A career field retention profile could provide useful insights into what the 1B4 profile will look like going forward.

Although we were able to explore enlisted retention in these figures, we were unable to explore retention of civilian personnel because of data limitations in the methods currently available to AFPC to identify civilians in the CMF through civilian personnel data files. We recommend that efforts be undertaken to improve AFPC's ability to identify and track civilians in the CMF by establishing identifiers in the USAF personnel data records in use by AFPC that can allow the retention of those personnel to be tracked over time.

Figure 3.6. Cumulative Continuation Rates of 1B4s, 1N4As, and USAF Overall

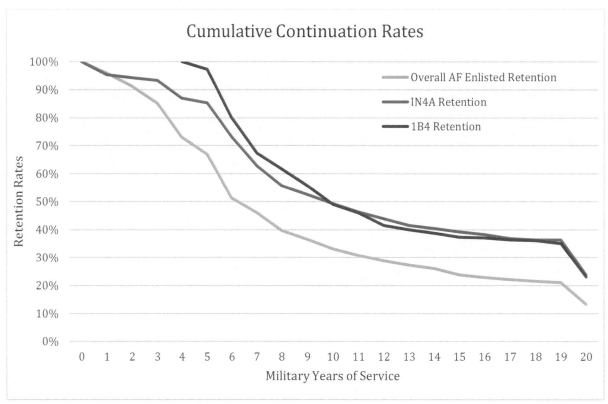

NOTE: Cumulative continuation rates were calculated using end-of-fiscal-year Air Force Active Enlisted personnel data files. We used fiscal year 2012 to 2018 files for the 1N4As, fiscal year 2011 to 2018 files for the 1B4s, and fiscal year 2011 to 2018 files for the "All Enlisted" category. The "All Enlisted" category includes all USAF specialty codes that begin with 1 to 7. *Cumulative continuation rates* are defined for each military year of service as the probability that an enlisted accession will remain on active duty through that year of service (definition derived from Military Leadership Diversity Commission, 2010).

Figure 3.7. 1B4 and 1N4A Cumulative Continuation Rates, by AFQT Quartile

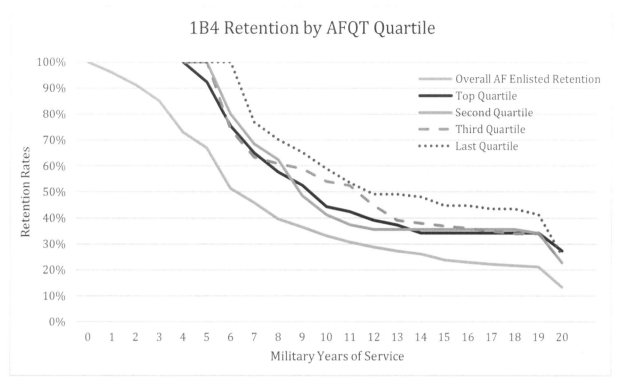

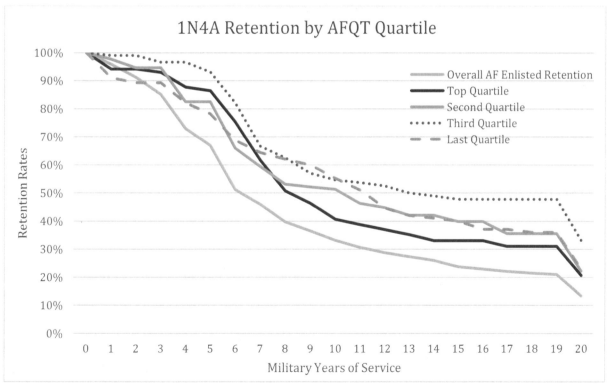

NOTE: 1B4 AFQT quartile ranges are as follows: first (top) = 93 to 99; second = 85 to 93; third = 75 to 85; and fourth (last) = 37 to 75. 1N4A AFQT quartile ranges are as follows: first (top) = 87 to 99; second = 76 to 87; third = 68 to 76; and fourth (last) = 36 to 68.

4. Recommendations

In this chapter, we recommend actions that USAF could take to help address the concerns raised by the members of the workforce who participated in our study.

Recommendations for Retaining and Recruiting USAF Cyber Personnel

The following recommendations reflect our view of the most-pressing concerns for recruiting and retention. Other recommendations certainly could follow from our findings.

Track and Monitor Retention, Especially of Top Performers

As noted previously, participants were most concerned about the loss of the best and the brightest (or, conversely, high retention of mediocre personnel) in all three of the groups of interest (1B4s, 1N4As, and CMF civilians). If it is true that these top performers are being lost, this could lead to major weaknesses in USAF's ability to outsmart its cyber adversaries. As a result, USAF should explore this issue further and monitor it going forward.

Unfortunately, USAF currently has no systematic way to identify or track top performers, mediocre performers, and poor performers for the purposes of confirming these concerns or monitoring retention among these personnel going forward. Therefore, we also recommend that USAF collect data that identify these top-performing personnel,[34] specifically for the purpose of tracking their retention. Such a data-collection effort would need to be executed in a way that encourages honesty about individuals' skills and capabilities rather than causing rating inflation, which can occur in data that are made available to or used by personnel in charge of assignment decisions or promotions. Keeping top-performer information separate from any personnel decision data sets would therefore be an important part of ensuring the success and validity of that effort. Although there certainly would be challenges, it is clear from discussions with the

---

[34] USAF has no clear way to identify its best performers for the purpose of tracking their retention. It is possible that the people who are considered the best performers by their peers and supervisors would appear unremarkable in the current performance evaluation system and would go unnoticed if personnel data alone were relied on in their current state. This could easily occur because there are plenty of incentives for personnel who are not the best cyber performers to receive higher performance ratings under the current system. This includes the fact that, as some participants noted, there are personnel who intentionally do poorly on their promotion tests to delay getting promoted and being moved into supervisory roles. Therefore, we recommend that additional research explore how best to identify and track high performers and that such identification and tracking be kept entirely separate from the performance appraisal and promotion system to encourage honesty about performance and preserve the validity of the data.

workforce that tracking retention of top personnel, and not just the overall number of personnel, is viewed as critical to ensuring that there are no retention problems in the cyber workforce.[35]

Develop Materials to Help Get Recruiters and the Public Well Versed in Cyber Career Fields

USAF recruiters face the difficult task of relaying critical information on a myriad of career fields to interested candidates entering the service. Although no single recruiter can be expected to know all of the career fields in depth, it is worth asking what more can be done to inform recruiters and incoming candidates about the cyber career fields so that they have a more realistic and complete picture of the rewards and rigors of the jobs. To help support better understanding both by recruiters and by applicants, we suggest developing materials (e.g., videos, handouts) that can be used to better explain the job to a lay audience and the overall criticality of the cyber mission to USAF. The goal for the materials should be to balance two seemingly competing goals. First, the materials should be aimed at providing a realistic job preview that includes discussion of the variety of skill, ability, and interest requirements (including that the job might require constant self-paced, self-directed, and self-initiated learning)[36] that is meant to ensure that people who are not suited for the job (and not likely to be happy or successful) are discouraged from applying. Second, the materials should be designed to get a much wider variety of people interested in the job, especially those who have never considered it and who have no expertise but who would still likely be successful.

Truncate the Onboarding Process for Civilians

Applicants with prior USAF service with cyber backgrounds who wish to come back as civilian cyber specialists face mandated hiring delays that, according to participants, can result in applicants reconsidering their interest and instead joining the private sector—a huge loss given the expertise they often bring with them. To help address this, methods aimed at truncating the onboarding process for civilians, without compromising on quality, ought to be considered. This includes DoD revisiting the statutory 180-day waiting period for opportunities to champion changes to the law.[37] Similarly, efforts should be made to expedite the clearance process, to the

---

[35] In exploring retention of cyber personnel, there is also a need to better understand and consider retention from a total-force perspective. If active-duty cyber personnel are leaving but returning as USAF reserve, guard, or civilian personnel, the loss would be different than if they were leaving USAF entirely. Understanding the flows of personnel across these groups could help identify alternative ways that USAF could achieve its mission using total-force initiatives at times when active-duty retention might be difficult.

[36] These are examples of requirements for success that we derived from respondents' comments.

[37] This 180-day processing period likely stems from federal hiring requirements and therefore might not be under the control of USAF policymakers. There is a 180-day rule that applies only to retiring military personnel transitioning to civil-service positions and not separating military personnel per the 2017 National Defense Authorization Act (effective December 23, 2016; see Public Law 114–328, 2016). Personnel falling under a special

extent possible. In addition, USAF should explore whether financial compensation could be made available to otherwise viable applicants while they are undergoing the clearance process to help protect against losing them to the private sector during that clearance waiting period. For example, offering temporary work duties in the interim might help address the gap in pay that would otherwise be incurred by these personnel.

Create Senior Technical Roles That Are Not Management Oriented

Participants talked about the need to find a way to keep personnel on keyboard to help address retention issues by allowing personnel to continue to do the work that they enjoy most,[38] and this applied to both civilians and enlisted personnel. Many participants noted that a warrant officer program for enlisted airmen would address this but pointed out that USAF has no such program currently. Although participants acknowledged that a warrant officer program might never be a possibility within USAF, many mentioned the benefits of having such a program.

Some noted that there could be ways to achieve the benefits that make a warrant officer program so attractive, specifically the ability to continually increase someone's pay but still allow them to remain on keyboard without requiring them to take on a leadership role. Finding a way to allow this ability for both civilians and enlisted personnel would be ideal.

As one example, a few participants mentioned that the Cyber Excepted Service will allow civilian members to receive merit-based pay increases without moving up in pay grade. If this option is offered to civilian cyber personnel widely, and if a similar program could be developed to address the same issue with enlisted personnel, it might prevent some of the issues that participants raised, including enlisted attempts to prevent promotion by intentionally failing Weighted Airman Promotion System tests or high-performing civilians and enlisted personnel being tempted to leave the service so that they can continue to spend time on keyboard.

Take Steps to Address Bureaucracy and Other Major Sources of Dissatisfaction

Participants discussed a wide variety of sources of dissatisfaction within their community, some of which they said was affecting retention. The level of bureaucracy in USAF and its impact on executing the mission was one such example. Other examples (e.g., in the write-in

---

salary rate table (such as air traffic controllers and IT managers) might also be exempt from the 180-day requirement. We recommend further confirming with AFPC the reasons for the 180-day policy affecting this career field, any constraints that AFPC might face in modifying it, and any current policy for handling waiver requests. In addition, USAF could explore whether there might be alternative total-force solutions to circumvent this 180-day waiting period (or any other similar civilian hiring obstacles), including, for example, onboarding affected personnel as reservists instead of civilians—although age maximums in the Air Force Reserve Command and Air National Guard might prevent such workarounds.

[38] This recommendation is discussed in both volumes of this report because participants discussed it as relevant both to maintenance of the workforce's technical skills and to reasons personnel might decide to separate from USAF.

responses) included not spending enough time on keyboard and leadership at multiple levels not understanding cyber.[39]

Although participants named many specific examples, it is this general frustration with the job that USAF likely really needs to address to make sure it can counter the draw of the private sector. Such issues as bureaucracy getting in the way of doing the work are not things that USAF can change quickly, but efforts can be made to start streamlining decisionmaking, educating leadership on what cyber is and how it can be used, and removing additional duties and training hurdles that prevent cyber personnel from getting the opportunity and time to do the work that they enjoy.[40] All of these obstacles, which are among the most commonly cited sources of dissatisfaction, are likely consequences of the fact that cyberwarfare has become so central to the USAF mission so quickly and have arisen as part of the resulting growing pains of the enterprise. The key to addressing them is for leadership to take steps now to ensure that they do not continue as the enterprise normalizes and becomes part of the status quo.[41]

Improve Identification and Tracking of Civilians in the Cyber Mission Force

Lastly, we faced various challenges in this project because there is currently no clear way of identifying members of the civilian workforce working in the CMF. Instead, we found that the civilians who make up this workforce come from a variety of civilian occupational codes, and only a small subset of the personnel in each of these codes is assigned to CMF-type work. This made recruiting participants a challenge, and it also hampered our ability to explore retention of these individuals in the civilian personnel data files. Without a clear code in the civilian personnel data files that identifies these individuals and is applied to them consistently, retention data will continue to be unavailable on this population. We therefore recommend that efforts be undertaken to improve AFPC's ability to identify and track civilians in the CMF by establishing identifiers in the USAF personnel data records in use by AFPC that can allow the retention of those personnel to be tracked over time.

---

[39] Participants described this as being an issue with USAF senior leaders, noncyber commanders in charge of making operational decisions, policymakers in charge of making personnel and resource decisions that affect cyber and noncyber leadership, in general, at all levels.

[40] Frustration with the imposition of additional duties is not a new phenomenon in USAF. In some critically manned career fields, leadership has found ways to limit these duties to protect airman time. Similar measures could be applied to this career field. Leadership typically is willing to explore limiting these duties as a temporary stopgap measure if the career field is facing manning shortages. It might be more difficult, however, to justify eliminating these additional duties if manning is not a problem, unless the career field can demonstrate that it is losing critical personnel to retention issues (i.e., if only the best and the brightest are leaving—and leaving in droves).

[41] Note that our participants identified some things as being potentially unnecessary that might still be important military practices that USAF might be unwilling to eliminate, such as wearing uniforms. The solution for these issues might be to better educate personnel on why these practices have value or are necessary in their career fields.

Some Final Notes on the Ongoing and Shared Challenges of Recruiting and Retaining Cyber Personnel

As explained in Chapter 1, USAF commissioned this study because it continues to be concerned about recruiting and retention in the cyberwarfare career fields; careers in these fields are both in high demand and mission critical. As shown in this report, our participants are concerned about these issues as well. It is worth noting, however, that these concerns are not new. Past research for USAF on cyber workforce retention (e.g., Hardison et al., 2019; Parker, 2016; Schmidt et al., 2015) shows that this has been an ongoing concern for leadership for several years, and we can see that USAF leadership has made continuous changes and adjustments to how the cyber workforce has been managed over that period that were informed by some of these studies. The results of this study are to be viewed similarly—as additional input to forward-looking policy changes that USAF could consider for addressing what the workforce views as real potential recruiting and retention problems, possibly before the full impacts of those problems are realized.

It is also worth noting that many of the concerns about hiring and retention of cyber personnel that our participants discussed in this study are not localized to USAF. For example, similar concerns about cyber workforce recruiting and retention issues have been explored in the U.S. Army (e.g., U.S. Government Accountability Office [GAO], 2019a; Wenger, O'Connell, and Lytell, 2017), the U.S. Marine Corps (e.g., Hernandez and Johnson, 2014), and the U.S. Navy (Bayer et al., 2019). In addition, a 2019 GAO report (GAO, 2019b) cited hiring and retaining key cybersecurity management personnel as a major concern among all 23 of the U.S. federal agencies that GAO included in its study. Although each of these organizations undoubtedly faces unique cyber workforce challenges, some of the concerns that we heard echo those reported from these other services and federal agencies (e.g., lengthy onboarding process for civilians, inability to compete with private-sector salaries). As a result, some of our recommendations might be similar to recommendations proposed in these other studies, and any efforts to address them might be relevant not only to USAF but also to some of these other organizations. Because there might be overlap in some of the challenges and the solutions across these groups, USAF might want to establish a leadership discussion forum for sharing ideas, issues, and lessons learned across these groups, if such a forum does not already exist.

Another point worth noting about the potential for shared recruiting and retention issues is that the OCO and DCO cyber communities are not the only USAF communities that are considered mission critical, facing constant ramp-up in demand, and concerned about recruiting and retention of their personnel. The remotely piloted aircraft community is one example of a workforce that has struggled to meet surges in demand by commanders while facing personnel shortages because of recruiting and retention challenges. Recent studies of that workforce have put forth various recommended approaches for addressing those challenges (e.g., Hardison et al., 2017; Terry et al., 2018). Other in-demand or undermanned communities that might have insights into useful recruiting and retention policy levers include the battlefield airmen and special tactics communities, other rated career fields (including pilots), and the intercontinental ballistic missile career fields. We therefore recommend that the USAF cyber community reach out to these other career fields for additional lessons learned.

Lastly, we note that although we explored past retention behaviors within the 1N4A and 1B4 career fields in the personnel data files, those data files reflect retention behaviors under the prior retirement system. With the recent introduction of the Blended Retirement System (BRS), there is now considerable uncertainty in how retention profiles will look going forward. Given that some personnel have opted into the BRS while others have not, it is likely that retention patterns will be affected, and the effects will likely continue to change and evolve over time. Research that continues to explore the impact of the BRS on retention in USAF in general or in other career fields might provide useful new insights for cyber retention.[42]

---

[42] For more on the BRS, see Asch, Mattock, and Hosek, 2017.

Appendix A. Focus Group Results, by Specialty

In Figures A.1 and A.2, we present results separately for each of our target specialty groups: 1B4s, 1N4As, and CMF civilians. We note again that sample sizes reported in these figures are small for the 1N4As (number of groups = 8) and especially so for the civilians (number of groups = 4). As a result, any differences between the groups should be viewed with great caution. That is, differences that appear large in the figure might in fact be insignificant, both statistically and practically, in any or all cases.

For example, having only four civilian discussion groups means that a difference of one group making or not making a particular point translates to a difference in 25 percent of the groups. If a topic was mentioned in one group, it equates to 25 percent in the figure, if it was mentioned by two, it equates to 50 percent; three equates to 75 percent; and four equates to 100 percent. By contrast, a difference of one group in the 1B4 discussions equates to a difference of only 6 percent. This means that, for the civilian data, it would be an overinterpretation of the data to suggest that something mentioned by four groups (100 percent) is a more widely held view than something mentioned by only three (75 percent). Because the sample is so small, we also cannot conclude that, if something was not mentioned in any of the four groups (0 percent), it is not a concern for the civilians.

Lastly, although the total numbers of *groups* are four, eight, and 18 for civilians, 1N4As, and 1B4s, respectively, it is important to note that the number of participants in each of those groups is larger (seven, 23, and 45, respectively). Although this helps lend additional strength to the data, the number of individuals in the civilian group is still small, and, for that reason, our caveats above (and elsewhere in this report) still stand.

Figure A.1. Percentage of Focus Groups That Mentioned Specific Topics About Recruiting, by Specialty

	1B4	1N4A	Civilian
	(number of groups = 18)	(number of groups = 8)	(number of groups = 4)
Discussed recruiting topic	94%	100%	100%
Yes, there are recruitment challenges	39%	63%	25%
No, there are not recruitment challenges	61%	63%	75%
Reasons offered			
Cyber is a desirable field	61%	38%	25%
Identifying appropriate personnel is a problem	50%	50%	25%
Long hiring or onboarding process is a problem	11%	13%	25%
Recruits' lack of intrinsic motivation (i.e., mission motivation) is a problem	17%	13%	0%
Recruits aren't aware of what cyber entails (not a recruiter issue)	6%	25%	25%

NOTE: Percentages represent the number of focus groups in which a topic was mentioned by at least one person.

Figure A.2. Percentage of Focus Groups That Mentioned Specific Topics About Retention, by Specialty

	1B4 (number of groups = 18)	1N4A (number of groups = 8)	Civilian (number of groups = 4)
Discussed retention topic	100%	100%	100%
Yes, there are retention challenges	72%	88%	75%
No, there are not retention challenges	17%	25%	0%
Reasons offered			
Industry competition presents challenges*	83%	75%	75%
Red tape issues are problematic	61%	25%	75%
Job dissatisfaction not related to red tape*	44%	38%	50%
Being pulled off keyboard (retention-related only)	50%	38%	0%
Poor motivation among cyber personnel	17%	0%	0%
Civilian development / promotion is a problem	0%	0%	75%

NOTE: Sometimes, a topic was raised by one person, and an opposite view was expressed by someone in the same discussion group. In those cases, the same discussion would be counted in both the topic frequency and the opposite sentiment frequency. For some topics, no opposite sentiment was expressed in the workforce discussions. When an opposite sentiment was expressed in more than 7 percent of the workforce discussions, it was added to the figure. Where an opposite sentiment was expressed in 3 to 7 percent of the workforce focus groups (i.e., one or two groups), the category is marked with an asterisk. Percentages represent the number of focus groups in which a topic was mentioned by at least one person.

Appendix B. Questionnaire Methodology

During the focus group discussions with members of the workforce, we administered a questionnaire.[43] The questionnaire consisted of a series of Likert-scale questions (i.e., on a scale of 1 to 5). For example, one question asked participants to rate their satisfaction with aspects of their career. In addition to the Likert-scale questions, participants were given two open-ended questions to which they were asked to provide written responses:

- What do you like most about your job as a cyber professional in your cyber workforce community?
- What do you like least about your job as a cyber professional in your cyber workforce community?

Finally, participants were asked to provide basic demographic information about their rank and pay grade, job type, and their training background. As shown in Table B.1, a total of 67 participants completed a questionnaire,[44] although some participants left questions blank. Notably, only seven respondents were civilians. Thus, mean scores on the questionnaire for civilians reported throughout this report should be interpreted with caution because the scores garnered from the small sample of respondents might not generalize to all civilians. Total number of respondents to each of the open-ended questions is shown in Table B.2.

Although participants were asked to attend a group for either OCO or DCO participants, depending on their work roles, we also asked participants to report their work roles on the questionnaire. As shown in Table B.1, that resulted in a different count for OCO and DCO representation than what we report for the focus group results. For example, some participants reported that their work contains both OCO and DCO roles, and many reported having another role as well. The "other" category includes written-in responses by the participants, such as "tech school," "intel support to national mission," "malware analysis," "finances," "not OCO/DCO," and "I have no expertise."

---

[43] Much of this section also appears in Hardison et al., 2021.

[44] The number of surveys completed is smaller than the number of discussion participants because those who participated over the phone were not administered questionnaires.

Table B.1. Number of Participants Who Responded to the Questionnaire

Type of Discussion	Sample Size
By specialty	
1B4	40
1N4A	20
CMF civilian	7
By base	
Fort Meade	40
JBSA	12
Scott Air Force Base	15
By self-reported work role	
DCO	27
OCO	25
Both OCO and DCO	9
Other (e.g., staff, finances, intel support) or unknown (e.g., not OCO/DCO)	6

Table B.2. Number of Write-In Responses, by Item

Values	1B4	1N4A	Civilian	Total
What do you like **least** about your job?	40	20	7	67
What do you like **most** about your job?	39	20	7	66
Please provide any additional comments.	8	8	5	21

References

Asch, Beth J., Michael G. Mattock, and James Hosek, *The Blended Retirement System: Retention Effects and Continuation Pay Cost Estimates for the Armed Services*, Santa Monica, Calif.: RAND Corporation, RR-1887-OSD/USCG, 2017. As of August 25, 2021: https://www.rand.org/pubs/research_reports/RR1887.html

Bayer, Michael J., John M. B. O'Connor, Ronald S. Moultrie, and William H. Swanson, *Secretary of the Navy: Cybersecurity Readiness Review*, Washington, D.C.: Headquarters, Department of the Navy, March 2019. As of April 12, 2021: https://www.wsj.com/public/resources/documents/CyberSecurityReview_03-2019.pdf?mod=article_inline

Bui, Anh T., "1st Non-Prior Service Airman Graduates CWO Course," U.S. Air Force, April 11, 2019. As of April 12, 2021: https://www.960cyber.afrc.af.mil/News/Article-Display/Article/1813072/1st-non-prior-service-airman-graduates-cwo-course/

GAO—*See* U.S. Government Accountability Office.

Hardison, Chaitra M., Julia Whitaker, Danielle Bean, Ivica Pavisic, Jenna W. Kramer, Brandon Crosby, Leslie Adrienne Payne, and Ryan Haberman, *Building the Best Offensive and Defensive Cyber Workforce*: Volume I, *Improving U.S. Air Force Training and Development*, Santa Monica, Calif.: RAND Corporation, RR-A1056-1, 2021.

Hardison, Chaitra M., Eyal Aharoni, Christopher Larson, Steven Trochlil, and Alexander C. Hou, *Stress and Dissatisfaction in the Air Force's Remotely Piloted Aircraft Community: Focus Group Findings*, Santa Monica, Calif.: RAND Corporation, RR-1756-AF, 2017. As of April 12, 2021: https://www.rand.org/pubs/research_reports/RR1756.html

Hardison, Chaitra M., Leslie Adrienne Payne, John A. Hamm, Angela Clague, Jacqueline Torres, David Schulker, and John S. Crown, *Attracting, Recruiting, and Retaining Successful Cyberspace Operations Officers: Cyber Workforce Interview Findings*, Santa Monica, Calif.: RAND Corporation, RR-2618-AF, 2019. As of April 12, 2021: https://www.rand.org/pubs/research_reports/RR2618.html

Hernandez, Lucas F., and Derek K. Johnson, *Designing Incentives for Marine Corps Cyber Workforce Retention*, Monterey, Calif.: Naval Postgraduate School, December 2014.

Military Leadership Diversity Commission, "Officer Retention Rates Across the Services by Gender and Race/Ethnicity," Arlington, Va.: U.S. Department of Defense Office for Diversity, Equity, and Inclusion, Issue Paper 24, March 2010.

Parker, William E., IV, *Cyber Workforce Retention*, Maxwell Air Force Base, Ala.: Air University Press, CPP–2, 2016. As of April 12, 2021:
https://apps.dtic.mil/dtic/tr/fulltext/u2/1030226.pdf

Public Law 114–328, National Defense Authorization Act for Fiscal Year 2017, December 23, 2016. As of August 25, 2021:
https://www.govinfo.gov/content/pkg/PLAW-114publ328/pdf/PLAW-114publ328.pdf

Salomon, Richard, "180-Day Civilian Hiring Restriction Reinstated for Military Retirees," U.S. Air Force, March 7, 2017. As of April 12, 2021:
https://www.afpc.af.mil/News/Article-Display/Article/1105235/180-day-civilian-hiring-restriction-reinstated-for-military-retirees/

Schmidt, Frank L., and John E. Hunter, "The Validity and Utility of Selection Methods in Personnel Psychology: Practical and Theoretical Implications of 85 Years of Research Findings," *Psychological Bulletin*, Vol. 124, No. 2, 1998, pp. 262–274.

Schmidt, Lara, Caolionn O'Connell, Hirokazu Miyake, Akhil R. Shah, Joshua William Baron, Geof Nieboer, Rose Jourdan, David Senty, Zev Winkelman, Louise Taggart, Susanne Sondergaard, and Neil Robinson, *Cyber Practices: What Can the U.S. Air Force Learn from the Commercial Sector?* Santa Monica, Calif.: RAND Corporation, RR-847-AF, 2015. As of August 25, 2021:
https://www.rand.org/pubs/research_reports/RR847.html

Terry, Tara L., Chaitra M. Hardison, David Schulker, Alexander C. Hou, and Leslie Adrienne Payne, *Building a Healthy MQ-1/9 RPA Pilot Community: Designing a Career Field Planning Tool*, Santa Monica, Calif.: RAND Corporation, RR-2018-AF, 2018. As of August 25, 2021:
https://www.rand.org/pubs/research_reports/RR2018.html

U.S. Government Accountability Office, *Cybersecurity: Agencies Need to Fully Establish Risk Management Programs and Address Challenges*, Washington, D.C., GAO-19-384, July 2019a. As of April 12, 2021:
https://www.gao.gov/assets/710/700503.pdf

———, *Future Warfare: Army Is Preparing for Cyber and Electronic Warfare Threats, but Needs to Fully Assess the Staffing, Equipping, and Training of New Organizations*, Washington, D.C., GAO-19-570, August 2019b. As of April 12, 2021:
https://www.gao.gov/assets/710/700940.pdf

U.S. Office of Personnel Management, "General Schedule Overview: General Schedule Classification and Pay," webpage, undated. As of March 31, 2020: https://www.opm.gov/policy-data-oversight/pay-leave/pay-systems/general-schedule/

Wenger, Jennie W., Caolionn O'Connell, and Maria C. Lytell, *Retaining the Army's Cyber Expertise*, Santa Monica, Calif: RAND Corporation, RR-1978-A, 2017. As of July 14, 2021: https://www.rand.org/pubs/research_reports/RR1978.html